Bessers & the Rolling Stone

Bessers & the Rolling Stone

A MEMOIR

GINA DAVIDSON

Bessers & the Rolling Stone is a work of nonfiction. Some names and identifying details have been changed.

Copyright © 2023 by Gina Davidson

ginabdavidson@gmail.com

All rights reserved.

No part of this book may be reproduced in any form or by any electronic or mechanical means, including information storage and retrieval systems, without written permission from the author, except for the use of brief quotations in a book review.

ISBN: 9798397320436

First Edition

Printed in the United States of America

Book cover design by Julia Sorrenti

Author photograph by Larry Davidson

For Cliff, Clint & Tara

A rolling stone gathers no moss.

— PROVERB

Contents

Introduction — xi

PART ONE
1. The Box — 3
2. Next of Kin — 9
3. I've Been Everywhere — 17
4. How the Animals Eat — 21
5. The Expectation — 33
6. The Sky was Crying — 39
7. I Wish You Well — 45
8. Ray of Sunshine — 51

PART TWO
9. The Crack in His Voice — 59
10. No Boats Today — 63
11. The Middle of the Mess — 71
12. A Frenzied Scrawl — 77
13. Eighth Street — 83
14. My Little Game — 89
15. The Tarnished Mirror — 95

PART THREE
16. I Have a Dad — 105
17. Three T's — 113
18. Please Hold — 119
19. What's Behind Your I? — 123
20. A Clipping in My Wallet — 131
21. The Trouble with the Law — 135
22. His Family Photo Album — 141

PART FOUR
23. Overlapping Lines — 151
24. Closer Than That — 159
25. Bridging the Gaps — 167

26. Making Room — 177
27. Ready or Not — 181
28. All I Wanted — 189
29. The Only Card I Had — 193

PART FIVE

30. No More Swiveling — 199
31. What Sucks Now — 207
32. No Perfect Crime — 213
33. Blue-Eyed Groupie — 219
34. A Few Steps Away — 225
35. Each Little Box — 231
36. The Father Wound — 239
37. Even His Liver — 245

PART SIX

38. Keeping Him Comfortable — 255
39. When He Left — 265
40. The Plans I Had — 277
41. The Rock — 283
42. Going Back Home — 295
Epilogue — 297

In Memoriam — 303
Resources — 305
Acknowledgments — 307
About the Author — 309

Introduction

In writing this book, I used my personal journals, diaries, letters, and recollections to present my truth to the best of my ability. I thank my brothers and my sister for sharing their memories with me, for reading (and rereading) the manuscript, and for allowing me to share their words and their stories along with mine.

Part One

CHAPTER 1
The Box

APRIL 2011

My dad has been in my closet for seven years. And I like it that way. Before his death, he moved unpredictably in and out of my life. Now I know right where he is all the time, and he can't go anywhere.

The container that holds him is just a bit larger than a cigar box and made of cheap brown plastic. It landed on my front porch in Tallahassee between Christmas 2003 and New Year's Day 2004. I don't know which day because I was two hours away from home that week, on an annual holiday trip to Seaside, Florida, with my husband, our two small children, and my in-laws.

During my time at the coast, my dad's remains traveled more than a thousand miles, from the winter chill of Sheboygan, Wisconsin, where he'd lived nearly all his fifty-nine years and where I'd grown up, to my sunbaked front porch in Florida. For the first sixteen years of my life, I'd loved my dad fiercely, and for the subsequent twenty, I'd lived mostly without him.

Though I knew his remains would be shipped to me, it was unsettling to see the brown box on our porch as we pulled into our driveway upon our return home. I hadn't been expecting any other package. I knew it was my dad.

I felt his presence immediately, as if he himself had arrived and had been waiting for us to get home—a home he'd never been to in a state he'd never visited.

I turned my gaze from the box to my husband's eyes.

"He's here," I said.

Larry nodded and brought our minivan to a stop halfway up the drive.

I looked to the backseat where our son and daughter were making toddler talk with each other. Ty was three; Jillian was one. My dad had never met them.

"Go ahead," Larry said.

I opened the door of our Sienna and stepped out into the cool evening air. Larry pulled the van into the garage as I headed down the front walkway toward the twin columns of our vaulted porch.

It had been three weeks since I'd made the decision for my dad to be cremated. I'd asked for his remains to be sent to me. Those decisions had been easy to make in the moment. There were no other viable options. But now, now things felt very real. He was no longer lying in a hospital bed hooked to machines. All that was left of him was lying in front of me, in the cheapest box the crematorium made. All that was left of him now belonged to me. It felt right that he was here, but what would I do with him? I hadn't thought that part through.

I sat on the top step of the porch, twisted around, and reached for the box behind me, pulling at it with my fingertips. It barely budged. He wasn't moving. I pictured my dad's rugged face, his piercing blue eyes, his dark blond hair, and I cocked my head at the thought of having to put more effort into our reunion.

I swiveled on my bottom to face the box head on, heaved it off the ground, and shifted it to the crook of my left elbow. Its warmth, gathered from the winter sun, radiated through the thin fabric of my jacket. It felt like a living thing.

Our porch light came on. I heard the front door unlock and Larry, Ty, and Jillian rustling around inside as they made themselves at home again.

I turned back to the setting sun. For a minute or so, I sat in silence staring out across our front lawn watching the light fade.

This is the end of our story, I thought.

My dad and I had last spent time together in October 1996. I was twenty-eight. He was fifty-two.

During the following seven-and-a-half years, there'd been no communication. Not a single call or letter. Not a word.

I'd come to a point where I'd expected someone to call me in the middle of the night to let me know he'd died. To tell me that he'd drunk himself to death.

I looked down at the box and ran my fingers along the smooth white duct tape that sealed one side. I read the return address on the index card taped to the top. It had come from Ballhorn Funeral Chapel in Sheboygan.

The contents of the box were listed as well.

My fingers touched on my dad's name, *Roy Earl Wilsing*, and his birthdate, *July 9, 1944*. I stopped. His birthday was July 19. I shook my head at the carelessness of the funeral home employee who'd made that typo and hadn't bothered to double-check.

I moved on to the date of his death, *December 18, 2003*. That had been the date the hospital staff had told me, so I'd assumed it was correct. An article in *The Sheboygan Press* had said it was December 19. I hadn't been there when he'd passed away, so I didn't know for sure.

That was it—a birth date and a death date, and ashes in a box. Was that all his life came down to?

He'd left behind no personal possessions to sift through or divvy up. Not a single thing. He'd had no car to sell. And I had no idea what had happened to his bent-up bicycle, the one he'd been riding at the time of the accident that had landed him in the hospital. I didn't know where he'd been living or where he'd spent his last night. No one I knew did.

I wrapped my arms around the warm little box. What now?

His final resting place should be in Sheboygan. He'd been born and raised there, had spent nearly all his life there. It was the right thing to do. But I didn't want to go there. I couldn't afford to go there. I couldn't afford a funeral or a memorial. I didn't know who would come anyway.

I looked back at the box.

I'm going to keep you here with me for a while, I said in my head to my dad. Maybe a few months was my thought, while I figured out what to do.

I was ready to rejoin Larry and the kids inside. I would need to bring my dad into my home—a thing I'd never done. I hoisted up the box and opened our front door.

Come on in, I said, picturing my dad beside me. *Make yourself at home.*

I walked through the house straight to our back room, our home office, where I'd been working just a few weeks before when the phone call had come telling me that my dad had been in an accident.

Not knowing what else to do with my dad's remains, I set the box on the floor of the closet.

That was seven years ago. My dad has stayed in that spot since the night he arrived. A bit longer than I'd anticipated. I realize it's not a proper resting spot, but no one's inquired or complained. His immediate family, his parents and three older brothers, had passed away years before he did, his two sisters-in-law had grown tired of his antics, and his three ex-wives had all remarried. My three half-siblings, all younger than I am, hardly knew him.

If I'd planned a service, some of them may have come, but I would've been the one to give the eulogy. If I'd planned a memorial, I would've been the one to gather old pictures and newspaper articles that highlighted his accomplishments—his athleticism in his youth, his talent as a floor installer, his voice when he sang and played guitar.

There were no flowers sent or music played in his honor. There should have at least been music. I could've played guitar. He'd taught me how when I was ten.

But I planned no service. Gave no eulogy. Did no gathering. I didn't even write an obituary. So no one did.

On the January evening his box arrived, I made the correction to his birthdate with a ballpoint pen, and then for more than seven years, left the box untouched. I can see it when I open the bi-fold closet doors. It's obscured by pictures, poster boards, files, and other items I haven't found a better home for, but every time I search for something or reorganize a bit, I catch a glimpse of it. I see him waiting.

I know it's time to let him go.

I just don't know how.

CHAPTER 2

Next of Kin

DECEMBER 9, 2003

It was an ordinary Tuesday evening, shortly after seven o'clock. I was typing in sales orders for work on the computer in our home office. Ty and Jillian were tucked in for the night and the only sound in our house was the faint stream of dialogue coming from our living room where Larry was watching *The West Wing*.

I remember the details of that December night as clearly as I remember where I was and what I was doing the January morning the Challenger exploded during my senior year, the August evening Princess Diana's car crashed in Paris, and the September morning the Twin Towers collapsed.

The unexpected ring of our home phone had startled me, and I jumped from my chair to grab the receiver so the noise wouldn't wake the kids. Flipping it over, I read the caller ID and froze in disbelief.

Sheboygan Memorial Hospital.

I intuitively knew why they were calling.

Though it had been more than seven years since I'd last

seen or spoken to my dad and I didn't know his address, I knew he was living in Sheboygan. And I knew he wasn't doing well.

One of his sisters-in-law, my Aunt Eunice, would see him once a week or so when he'd stop by her house. Typically, he arrived drunk. Always by bicycle, his only means of transportation.

Eunice knew he'd stopped communicating with me. She and I corresponded by letter, and she would let me know when he stopped by. She told me he read the family letter I sent to her each Christmas. It made me happy to know that at least he knew I'd married Larry and that we'd had two children, but it made me sad that he knew and he still didn't reach out. My Aunt Eunice was our only link.

I hit the button to answer the call. Unnerved by the idea that my premonition was coming true, I brought the receiver to my face and whispered hello.

"Hello," a woman's gentle voice answered in response. She confirmed she was calling from Sheboygan Memorial Hospital. "I'm trying to locate Gina Beth Wilsing. Are you Miss Wilsing?"

I sucked in a breath.

"Yes, that's me. That's my maiden name." There was only one reason they would use it. This was definitely about my dad. They were going to tell me he was dead.

I'd thought I'd be ready to hear it when the time came, but now I wasn't so sure. After years of an on-again, off-again relationship with him, I hadn't known what else to do to stay connected. I'd given up trying and had told myself I was okay with that.

The ceiling fan whirred above me. I glanced at the clock on my desk. 7:20.

"Do you know a Roy Wilsing?" the woman asked.

My hand went to my mouth. The reality of the moment

shook me. Had I willed for this to be the end? Had I contributed to it somehow?

"Yes," I said, and waited. I leaned on the table in front of me, afraid my legs would collapse beneath me when she told me his life was over. I had only wanted the pain of our estrangement to end.

"Are you his daughter?"

His daughter. It had been so long since I'd thought of myself as that.

"Yes," I answered, to keep things uncomplicated.

Time seemed to slow down. Stop.

Just tell me.

"Miss Wilsing, your father's been in an accident and is in an unstable condition."

It took a moment to process what she'd said.

Unstable condition? What exactly did that mean? He wasn't dead, but he might die?

"We need your consent to transport him by ambulance to Froedtert Medical Hospital in Milwaukee where they can provide the care he needs."

My consent? Why do they need my consent?

"We need to go over the possible risk factors associated with his transfer," she said.

Our conversation was so matter-of fact. As I listened to her words, I tried to wrap my head around the fact that my dad was still alive.

"His condition could deteriorate, possibly impacting his heart and brain function and adding to his nerve damage," the woman went on. "There could also be increased bleeding and further damage to the surrounding tissues."

My mind reeled. I crossed back to the swivel chair in front of my desk and sat down. The computer, the piles of paper, the room—everything began to lose definition.

I was relieved to know my dad was actually alive and that

things hadn't ended the way I'd thought they would. I pictured him in an ambulance being whisked to Milwaukee.

"Do we have your consent?" the woman asked.

"Of course. Of course," I stammered. Why were they asking me? Surely there was someone closer to him, nearby, who could give consent.

"Ma'am, do you have a pen and paper? I need to give you more information."

"Yes," I said, but no, I didn't.

My fingers fumbled for the pen on my desk, and I grabbed a pad of seasonal stationery that was nearby. Below an illustration of two snowmen and a banner that read, "What I Want for Christmas," I scribbled the phone number the woman gave me and jotted down the name of a trauma nurse at Froedtert: *Sally*. The pen in my hand continued scrawling words, but my brain was not registering their meaning: *ER... unconscious... ICU... bleeding in brain...*

I absentmindedly retraced the letters I'd written as she continued. My mind returned to the fact that she'd called to get my consent.

"How'd you get my number?" I asked. During the previous seven years, Larry and I had moved from Florida to North Carolina and back again. Surely my dad hadn't carried my number in his wallet. Or had he?

"Eunice Wilsing is listed as a contact for him," she replied. "She gave it to us."

"Oh," I said, saddened to realize that if it hadn't been for my Aunt Eunice, the hospital may not have been able to track me down.

"She said you're next of kin."

Whatever had been left of the world I once knew fell away with those words. I was stunned. It had never occurred to me that I was next of kin, but once she said it, it made perfect sense. Of course I was next of kin. I was his *only* kin. Well, technically, my dad had had four children, but I was the oldest and the only one who called him Dad.

"You can call Froedtert in a couple hours," the woman continued. "Sally will have more details for you."

Right, I thought, *because I'm next of kin.*

Holy shit, I'm next of kin.

"Your father will be transferred to their Neurological Intensive Care Unit. Nurse Sally will want to talk with you. You can let her know when to expect you."

My breath caught in my throat. *Expect me?*

"Oh-kay," I said, and then she was gone.

I hung up and sat perfectly still in my chair. I needed a moment to assemble this onslaught of information.

They *expect* me?

An image of my dad came to mind—from the last time I'd seen him, in the fall of 1996 when Larry and I had traveled to Sheboygan for my ten-year class reunion. Larry met my dad then for the first time. At the end of our visit, Larry suggested taking a picture of us, and my dad and I had posed side-by-side in front of the house a friend was letting him stay in on Tenth Street near Lake Michigan. My dad put his arm around my shoulder and stood proudly next to me. It was the closest I'd been to him in a decade.

For our first visit in ten years, I'd dressed in a nice black turtleneck, plaid flannel shirt, and new pair of jeans. My dad had donned a tattered red t-shirt with a hole near the hem and beige bell-bottoms that hung on his hips. We looked so alike with our dark blond hair, tanned skin, and light eyes, yet we were worlds apart.

I hadn't known it would be our last picture together. I hadn't known that the Christmas card I would send just a few months later to that same address on Tenth Street would come back stamped *Return to Sender, Address Unknown*, or that it would be the last address of his I would ever have.

After that visit, my annual Christmas letter to Aunt Eunice became the only means of communication between us. After a couple years, I willed myself to accept that. He knew what was happening in my life. He didn't reach out, but there was still a connection between us. I'd let that be enough for six years.

At the bottom of the Christmas letter I sent to Aunt Eunice in 2002, I added a small note just for him.

Tell him I said hello, I'd written, knowing he would see it. *Life is too short.*

He hadn't responded.

Now, within the hour, he would be heading to Milwaukee in critical condition. Life seemed shorter than ever.

But I should let Nurse Sally know when to expect me? That seemed extreme. Surely I could take care of things from Florida, by phone. I had two young children. I couldn't just up and leave.

The truth was I didn't want to. It had been disconcerting enough to see the condition my dad had been in in 1996. I didn't want to see what seven more years of drinking, hard living, and this accident had done to him. The harder truth was that I didn't want to plunge myself back into a cycle of caring too much and getting nothing in return. It hurt to hope.

I shook my head to readjust, turned back to the computer, and set my fingers on the keyboard, thinking I would pick up my work where I'd left off. But my fingers sat frozen on the keys. My eyes couldn't read the words on the screen, not because tears got in the way—there strangely were none—but because the world had warped into something unimaginable, just like when the Challenger blew up, Princess Di died, and the Twin Towers fell.

Unstable means he's not dead.
Unstable.
Not dead.

I sat up straighter, unsure of what to do with this information.

Maybe he'll be fine. Maybe when I called Froedtert, they'd say, "We're sorry, there's been a mistake. We'll take care of him. Sorry to have bothered you."

But maybe they wouldn't. Maybe they'd still want me to come.

I stood up on unstable feet. The whirring of the ceiling fan reentered my consciousness, and I once again could hear the rapid-fire dialogue coming from the TV in the living room. My home looked and sounded the same as it had before the call had come, but it was also eerily different—somehow unreachable. I was no longer able to tether myself to the world I'd lived in just an hour before.

CHAPTER 3
I've Been Everywhere

APRIL 1976

One of my first memories is of a bumblebee. Not of my parents getting divorced in 1972, when I was four, nor of my mom marrying my stepdad, Charlie, when I was five. Not of suddenly having a stepbrother, Rick, a year younger than I was, nor of my half-brother, Brett, being born when I was almost seven. But of a bumblebee, buzzing around me at a busy intersection in a suburb of Minneapolis near the house I moved into in second grade. I was eight years old.

I remember teetering on the yellow-painted curb beneath my feet, my pigtails flying in the wind, the sun warming my face, when a bumblebee unexpectedly flew in my path. Not at all concerned about the traffic whipping by on the four-lane road next to me, I flailed my arms to shoo the bee away and slipped into the street. I can still hear the startling blare of a semi's horn as it flew past me signaling danger. I can still remember what it felt like to be that little girl.

My parents' divorce, my mom's remarriage, and my stepdad's career ambitions had led to frequent changes in my life. The pale-blue two-story house I lived in with my mom, my stepdad Charlie, and Brett was right up the hill from the corner of the busy intersection where I'd encountered the bee. It was the eighth house I'd called home in my eight years.

During my kindergarten year, I'd gone to three different elementary schools in two different cities in Wisconsin. My mom and I lived with her mom, my Gramma Joe, in Manitowoc, for several months after the divorce. We then moved into a place of our own around the corner and then into Charlie's apartment in nearby Fond du Lac after she married him. During my first-grade year, they built a house together there, and we celebrated two Christmases in it before moving to Minnesota near the end of my second-grade year. Charlie's son Rick stayed in Wisconsin and was living with his mom and new stepdad. He would visit us each month.

The frequent changes were hard on me. Over and over again, I had to adjust—to new teachers, new schools, new cities—and all of that on top of a new stepdad, new stepbrother, and baby brother.

And then there was the adjustment of not getting to spend time with my dad on the weekends. Even though I'd moved from city to city, and he'd also moved—back to Sheboygan, the town I'd been born in—he'd always lived within an hour of me, and he'd pick me up on the weekends to stay with him at Grandma Wilsing's house.

Minneapolis was five hours from Sheboygan—way too far for my dad to travel back and forth twice in one weekend. I didn't see him even once during the year we lived there, and I missed our time together.

In later years, my stepdad would tell me that my dad didn't want to let me move to Minneapolis. He knew he wouldn't have the time or financial resources to be able to come see me.

But Charlie was in training to become a district manager for a nationwide insurance company, and he needed to move to Minneapolis to complete the program. My mom needed my dad's permission to let me live out-of-state. Charlie said he convinced my dad that it was in my best interest for us to move, and they settled things over a six-pack. I assumed he told me this to show how easily my dad could be swayed, but it also felt like he was telling me how little I was worth to my father. I knew better.

During my year in Minnesota, I managed to adjust again and made new friends, but I missed my dad. I missed my Grandma Wilsing and my aunts, uncles, and cousins. I was the only one missing from the bunch. So I was thrilled to learn in the middle of my third-grade year that Charlie's training was complete, and his new job would be taking us—of all places—back to Sheboygan. He would become the district manager he wanted to be, and I would once again get to live near my dad. He'd be right across town, and I looked forward to all the things we would get to do together again.

We'd once again make late-night Rocky Road sundaes with extra chocolate sauce in Grandma's tall dessert dishes, and my dad would stop at Piggly Wiggly on the way to her house to buy our horoscope scrolls. He'd read them aloud (Cancer for him, Aries for me) while we rocked on the large aluminum swing on Grandma's front porch.

We'd go up to his attic rooms, his bedroom and his living room, where he'd set up a stage for himself. He'd adjust his amps, put the mic on its stand, tune his electric guitar, and sing his favorite songs for me again. I already knew most of the words to "Garden Party" by Ricky Nelson, "It Was Almost Like a Song" by Ronnie Milsap, and "I've Been Everywhere" by Asleep at the Wheel. I would sing backup to "The Cover of The Rolling Stone," by Dr. Hook.

After all the moves and living so far away from my dad for

an entire year, I wanted nothing more than to get back to familiar territory. To live in Sheboygan. To go back to Eighth Street. To be my dad's little girl again. I expected things to go back to the way they had been.

How was I to know nothing would ever be the same again.

CHAPTER 4
How the Animals Eat

APRIL 1977

When I'd left Wisconsin during my second-grade year, my dad had been single. He'd seemed to be in no hurry to remarry like my mom had. I don't even remember him having a girlfriend. It had been just the two of us—plus Grandma—and that was fine by me.

Upon moving back, I abruptly discovered things had changed.

"You'll like her," he said of a woman named Debra. "She's fun!"

We were back together for the first time and in his car headed to meet her. I wasn't excited about this new development.

I'd been prepared to be the new kid in class—again—as my third-grade year was ending, and I'd known I'd be moving again before my fourth-grade year began, from the duplex my mom and Charlie were renting to the house they were buying. But I wasn't ready for an adjustment of this kind. I definitely knew I didn't want to share my dad.

At first, I did like Debra, despite not wanting to. And she was fun—mostly because she was so different from my mom and my dad and Charlie. For starters, she was just twenty years old, more than a decade younger than any of them, barely older than my babysitters, which was immediately cool.

She wore tight jeans and high black leather boots. She smoked cigarettes and cursed under her breath and didn't seem to care what anyone thought of any of it. She rode a Harley, owned a 35mm camera, and was enrolled in a black-and-white-photography class at the junior college in town.

One breezy spring day shortly after we met, she took me along on a photo assignment to the shore of Lake Michigan, a block behind Grandma's house. She pointed out the tips of the waves in the lake, the contrast between the dark water below and the foamy white crests. She noted budding leaves on the trees and snapped pictures of every detail.

That afternoon, she took me to the darkroom on her college campus. By the soft glow of a red light, I inched my way past pans half-filled with water as she unloaded the film from her camera.

"It's a safelight," she explained, pointing to the red bulb. "It won't mess up the prints. White light does." She was so smart, filling me in on stop baths, fixers, and how you wash a photo.

"You wash a photo?" I laughed.

She smiled. "Yep, and then you just rinse it and hang it up to dry." She clipped eight-by-ten pictures of the lake to the clothesline that hung diagonally near the ceiling of the room. I could see every detail she'd mentioned as we'd walked along the lakeshore. The rolling waves and sprouting leaves looked different, clearer, in black and white, and I was so intrigued by her knowledge of how it all worked.

I would see her every weekend when my dad picked me up for a visit, usually staying over a night or two at their place. Though we spent some enjoyable time together in the beginning, I'm not sure I can say that I ever loved Debra. Maybe because things changed so quickly, I never quite got the chance.

Debra, at twenty, was a bad ass. Full of possibilities. She was everything that my nine-year-old self never could have imagined being—fearless, fiercely independent, unapologetic.

Then she got pregnant.

During her third trimester, she married my dad. She was twenty-one, and he was thirty-three. My second half-brother, Cliff, was born a month after their wedding.

My dad was an alcoholic by then, but I didn't recognize this at my age. Maybe Debra didn't either. Years later, I would learn that she'd wanted out of their marriage early on, but soon she was pregnant again—with Clint, who was born fifteen months after Cliff. My guess is that she stayed until she just couldn't any longer.

I was eleven when Clint was born and understood nothing about how the responsibility of taking care of children could affect a marriage. I only knew there were no more walks along the lakeshore and no more talk of photography. Fun Debra was gone.

I continued visiting on the weekends. I loved snuggling with my baby brothers. Rocking them. Feeding them. Playing with them. I stole only mere moments with my dad, mostly on the car trips to and from their house. I don't remember any music during that time. No guitar playing or singing. I distinctly remember there being a tense stillness in the air all the time.

My dad joked around less. Smiled less. Paid less attention to me. He walked a fine line between being himself, laughing and being silly, and being the husband and father Debra expected him to be.

And then, she interjected herself in our relationship too.

It had long been a tradition for my dad to give me a dollar

every weekend he saw me. It was just a little something. But it felt like a token of love.

At the end of a weekend visit shortly after Clint was born, he handed me a dollar as we headed down the driveway to his car for him to take me home. I'd already said goodbye to Debra, Cliff, and Clint inside the house, and my dad and I had walked out alone. As soon as the dollar hit my fingers, I heard the screen door behind us fly open and turned around to find Debra standing on the front porch, hands on her hips, glaring at us.

"I expect you'll put a dollar in each of the boys' piggy banks when you get home," she yelled at my dad. Then she turned, went back inside, and let the screen door slam shut behind her.

The divide between us grew with every weekend visit that followed. Debra was always busy with the boys, making meals, being a mom. I didn't know where I fit in and mostly just tried to stay out of her way. Over the course of the next six months, my visits dwindled down to every other weekend, then either Friday or Saturday night, not both.

One Saturday afternoon, when the boys were just shy of one and two years old, more than the usual trepidation flooded through me as my dad drove me to their home. They'd recently moved into an old farmhouse they were renting on the outskirts of town, and I hadn't visited for a few weeks while they'd settled in. I was relieved by the break because before the move I'd spent the night and had accidentally left my diary behind. And Debra had read it.

She'd called to tell me so.

"You're a very angry girl," she'd said on our call after letting me know she'd found it.

I was in the sixth grade and had all the angst that came with being that age. In my diary, I'd poured out my unfiltered adolescent thoughts, my highest highs, my lowest lows. I'd written to my diary as if it were my best friend and spilled daily details about everything—the boys I liked, the friends I had, who'd gone roller skating Friday night, what chores I had to do. But most alarming to Debra, I'm sure, was that I'd written I hated both my stepparents.

Debra hadn't called to talk about my feelings though or to see how she could make things better somehow. She simply wanted to let me know she was aware of how I felt.

I felt sick.

Shortly after my dad and I arrived at their farmhouse that Saturday, Debra asked my dad to run to the store for a few items. I made a beeline to the boys, who were playing on the living room floor, and eventually lost myself in drawing on a large pad of paper with colorful markers I'd found on a high shelf.

Debra followed me into the room and played with the boys once I started to draw. Neither of us mentioned the diary. Or made eye contact.

After a long, awkward silence, she gestured to my drawing pad and asked, "Can I have a piece?"

I looked up, surprised she was engaging with me. Her face was a blank slate, and I was unsure of what she was up to. Was she trying to be nice? I carefully tore off a sheet and offered it to her.

She sized it up and then in thick, black marker drew large, curvy letters that spelled out my first name. It took up most of the space on the page. I watched as she picked up brightly colored markers and filled in each letter, one with polka dots, another with stripes, and so on.

I don't remember any conversation, not about the diary, nor about my dad, who I desperately wanted to walk in the door any second. I just remember the waiting and that Debra seemed to be softening.

Then a couple hours passed.

Debra made no mention of my dad, but I could tell she was irritated that he still hadn't returned.

She fed the boys an early dinner, and I helped tuck them in for the night, kissing their soft, downy hair and wondering where our dad could be.

Debra went to the kitchen to make dinner for us. I sat at the table and stared out the window to the driveway in the back of the house. Still, she didn't mention my dad's absence.

Except for the red spaghetti sauce she was cooking, I remember everything being white that night—the lace curtains that hung from a brass rod above the wide window, and beyond it, the snow layered on top of everything outside. The laminate flooring, her fitted crewneck t-shirt, the three dinner plates she stacked next to the stove.

Each time she turned her back to me, I'd glance at the gravel driveway outside the window, hoping to see the headlights of my dad's car, but all I saw in the fading light was their big, weathered barn in the backyard, standing empty, with icicles that had dripped into long, sharp points, refreezing as the temperature dropped.

I watched Debra move around the room, adding spices, sipping the sauce, draining the pasta. She was quiet, but at least she was being nice.

Finally, headlights shone through the window, and then went out. I heard the car door slam shut and my dad's heavy footsteps coming up the walkway that led to the kitchen, snow crunching under his boots as he made his way to the door. It swung open, and his face lit up when he saw me at the kitchen table.

"Bessers . . ." he said, drawing out the nickname he'd given me years before. He'd put his own spin on my cousin's mispronunciation of my middle name. "Beth" had come out "Bess," and then "Bessers" had stuck. He was the only one who called me that.

The winter wind had blown in with him, and his face was flushed. He turned to shut the door, then swung back and smiled at me. Debra stopped stirring the sauce at the stove and turned toward him. The softness I'd seen in her face while she'd colored and cooked had hardened. He hiccupped, stumbled a bit, and grabbed the doorknob to steady himself. It was the first time I'd seen him act this way. He wasn't quite himself.

"You've been gone for hours." Debra held him in a cold stare. "You just needed to go to the store."

"I ran into some buddies of mine," he said. "We just had a few drinks." He shrugged. "I'm here now. Man, it smells good in here!" He patted his stomach with both hands to show he was ready to eat.

He plopped down on the chair next to mine and gave me a wink.

"Hi, Bessers." He smiled.

I smiled.

"Ready for dinner?" he asked.

"She's been ready," Debra responded before I could. "We've been waiting. Go wash up."

My dad got to his feet, found the Ivory soap in a dish by the sink, and washed his hands. She watched him as he half-dried them on the white kitchen towel hanging nearby. He turned toward me, winked again, and sat back down.

Debra took a deep breath. I watched as she loaded a dinner plate with a mound of pasta and rich, red spaghetti sauce. She set it in front of my dad and then put a smaller portion on a second plate and set it in front of me. I lifted my fork from the table, ready to eat as soon as Debra was seated with her own plate.

"Hey Bessers, wanna see how the animals eat?" My dad was holding the sides of his plate with both hands.

"Sure," I said, curious as to what he was going to do.

He lifted his plate a few inches off the table and leaned his face in until his nose was practically touching the marinara. He gave me a sideways glance and raised his eyebrows in anticipation.

Debra let out a small laugh, despite her earlier hostility, and I thought, oh, good, everything's going to be okay. But then her icy white fingers slid under his plate, and she quickly pressed his dinner into his face.

The next several seconds were a furious blur. The plate fell from his face. His fist hit the table.

Debra flew to the phone on the wall and grabbed it. She tucked into the pantry and slammed the door behind her.

I watched in shock as my dad hurled his plate of spaghetti at it. Shards of white porcelain shot out. Red sauce slid down from the spot where the plate had struck.

I sat frozen in my chair, my fork still in my hand.

"Damn you!" he yelled at her. "What'd you have to go and do that for?"

She didn't answer, but I could hear her crying and mumbling into the phone between sobs.

"Debra!" he shouted toward the door. "Come out here!"

"No!" she shouted back. "I'm on the phone! Leave me alone!"

I looked at him, but he didn't look at me. Instead, he looked at the sauce dripping down the front of his shirt. He went to the sink and grabbed the white towel, turning his back on the pantry for a moment.

Debra darted out of the pantry, sped through the living room, and ran up the stairs to the second floor. My dad, looking like a lion charging after its prey, raced after her—his steps larger, his stride longer. His feet pounded down the hallway above, and my thoughts turned to Cliff and Clint who were sleeping up there. I ran through the living room but stopped at the base of the stairs. What did I think I could do?

I heard muffled voices coming from the room my dad shared with Debra, and I knew he'd gotten to their door before she could close it. A hard slap followed. Then nothing.

Within seconds, he thudded back down the stairs, whisked past me, and headed into the kitchen. The back door swung open and smacked shut. His engine started and I heard his car tear across the gravel.

Then the house was silent—as it had been before he'd come home, only worse. What had just happened? Who was that? I'd never seen him so mad.

Within seconds, I heard the faint sound of crying come from upstairs. At first I thought it might be the one of the boys, but it wasn't. It was Debra. I envisioned her holding a pillow over her face. Maybe so I wouldn't hear her. Maybe so she wouldn't wake the boys. Somehow, they'd slept through it all.

In that moment, I knew I was all she had. I had to check on her. Comfort her. I started up the stairs, each step leading me closer to a place I didn't want to go. I padded softly down the narrow hallway, past the boys' bedroom, and stood outside of hers. The door was flung wide open, a gaping entrance to a deep, dark cave I was afraid to go in. I stepped into the blackness anyway and saw the shape of her body beneath the covers on the bed. A sliver of her face was visible against her pillow. The top of her blanket covered everything except her eyes. I stepped in closer, but not too close. I cleared my throat, so she'd know I was there. Maybe I didn't have to say anything at all. She shifted her body and pulled her blankets further up, covering her head completely. Maybe I did.

"Are you . . . okay?" I managed to ask.

Silence. The blanket moved ever so slightly.

"Yeah," she breathed.

I hesitated before I said the next words that formed in my head. They'd been circling there since I'd heard the slap.

"Did he . . . ?"

Silence. She gathered the blankets more tightly around her.

"No," she said.

Would she tell me if he had?

"Okay," I said. I didn't really want to know. There was no part of me that could imagine my dad—my funny, loving, wonderful dad—would ever hurt anyone. Maybe that wasn't what I heard, I reasoned. I decided to believe her.

I made my way back downstairs and sank into their soft brown sofa, pulling a fuzzy maroon blanket around myself to keep warm. Glancing toward the kitchen floor, I could see splatters of dried spaghetti sauce and pieces of white porcelain, everything frozen in time, lying right where it had landed. I closed my eyes and drifted off, hoping that when I woke up everything would somehow be normal again.

Unfortunately, I'd see this same pattern play out during a visit just two weeks later, on Cliff's second birthday. My dad and Debra would argue. My dad would leave. Debra would run to their bedroom, slam the door shut, and cry into her pillow. The boys, again, happened to be sleeping. They'd gone down for a nap before the argument erupted, and they'd remained asleep. Maybe they were used to the commotion.

Once again, I sat alone on the living room couch. This time with the realization that this was how they lived. This was who he was with her. This was what life with my dad had become and would continue to be.

Once again, I was the only one left to comfort her. But this time, I didn't want to.

Once again, I was waiting for my dad to return. But I didn't want to do that either.

I just wanted to leave. But how could I call and ask my mom to come get me without telling her why?

I hadn't said a word to her or my stepdad Charlie about the spaghetti fight. I knew they already looked down on my dad.

He'd never been "responsible," according to my mother. It was the reason she'd left him after seven years of marriage. They'd been young—eighteen and twenty—and in love, but she'd needed more stability than he could provide. Even now, he was continually in and out of jobs, and he didn't make anything close to the money Charlie made.

My mom and Charlie had shook their heads when they'd learned Debra was pregnant and again when my dad had married her. I didn't want them to know things weren't working out. Calling her felt like the worst thing I could do. Like I was betraying my dad.

But I was scared, and I didn't feel safe, so I called anyway.

Cliff and Clint would wake to find me gone. Debra would come out and likely wonder where I was. And my dad would probably be concerned about me when he got back to the house and saw that I'd left, but I couldn't stay.

My mom and Charlie picked me up, and once I was home with them, I told her why I'd asked her to come. I had to let go of what she and Charlie would think. I had to hope my dad would understand.

I don't know if my leaving that day even registered on his radar. He may have checked on me. He may have called my mom. But his relationship with Debra was deteriorating at a rapid pace, and he had bigger things to worry about.

He didn't call to pick me up for several weeks, and by the time he did, before Clint's first birthday in April 1980, Debra had moved out. My dad had moved back to Grandma's on Eighth Street and began picking up Cliff and Clint on the weekends, right before he'd come to get me.

His divorce from Debra was final in October of that year, but she wasn't through with him yet. Before she left his life for good, she'd present him with an ultimatum, and his choice would cost us both.

CHAPTER 5

The Expectation

DECEMBER 9, 2003

Larry and I sat facing each other on the couch in the dim light of our living room. We'd turned off *The West Wing* and I'd relayed the details of my dad's condition based on what the nurse from Sheboygan had told me. It was just before eight o'clock in the evening.

"She said I should call Froedtert Hospital in a couple hours," I told Larry. "He should be there by then."

I didn't mention that the nurse expected me to come.

"Are you okay?" Larry asked, holding his hands out to me.

I shook my head and shrugged, unable to process what was happening. Unsure of what I felt. Relief that he was alive? Scared that he might die? Worried that I'd have to act as next of kin?

"I'm sure everything'll be fine," I said, diverting the conversation from myself.

I focused on what I might learn when I called. Would everything indeed be fine? Would I possibly be released from my newfound title of next of kin because my "services" wouldn't be needed? Because my dad's condition turned out to be less serious than they'd thought, and there'd be no need for me to be part of this?

After hardly being in his life for twenty years, it didn't seem right that I should be the one responsible for him. I had my own life, my own responsibilities. In order to be there for him, I'd have to leave my home, my kids, my new job, and Larry, who'd just started his new job. Not to mention it was two weeks before Christmas. It was unfair to be put in a position where I was expected to do anything after my dad had been absent from my life for so long.

I secluded myself in our home office at nine-thirty to make the call. Larry went to our room to get ready for bed. He had work in the morning.

I mentally crossed my fingers and hit the buttons to dial. How I hoped my dad could get the care he needed at Froedtert, and Nurse Sally would tell me I didn't need to come.

His transfer was complete, she told me when I reached her. My dad was in Froedtert's Neurological Intensive Care Unit.

"He has multiple traumas," she said.

"Yes," I said, and waited.

"He hasn't opened his eyes or responded to pain since the accident, but he did wiggle his thumb when asked to."

A flutter of hope ran through me, and I willed her to say the words I wanted to hear, *That's a good sign. He'll be fine. We'll take it from here.*

Instead, disregarding the thumb he'd wiggled, she let loose a string of details regarding the severity of his condition. My mind caught only fragments. I listed them on the lines of my snowman stationery, my hope of not being needed dwindling with each word:

fractured skull
right side of brain
fractured spine

no movement
paralyzed left side
ventilator
chance of survival - 20 to 30%
if bleeding continues, operate

She stopped speaking. I scribbled the last line, bewildered by all I'd heard.

"What happened?" I asked.

A car accident, she told me. According to the police report, he'd driven his bicycle into the side of a moving car. He'd flown off and his head had hit the windshield with no helmet to protect it.

I tried to imagine the scene. How could he have been riding a bike fast enough to cause that kind of damage? And then I thought of him riding a bicycle in December, through the freezing cold on snow-covered streets.

"There's bleeding in his brain," Nurse Sally continued. "His doctors will place tubes to drain the fluid and relieve some pressure." She paused. "You'll want to meet with them when you arrive. When can we expect you?"

There it was. The question. The expectation. I was needed as next of kin, and I'd have to make a choice.

I looked at the list I'd written on my stationery. The illustration of the two snowmen struck me. One was big and one was little—a mother, or maybe a father, and a child. I suddenly felt angry. I didn't want to be pulled back into his circle only to wind up disappointed again. I'd finally—after nearly a decade—accepted things as they were. I didn't want to start the cycle over.

"I'll have to call you back," I heard myself tell the nurse before I ended the call.

I rose from the office chair to make my way back to Larry. The air felt too thick to walk through. I got to our bedroom and cracked open the door. A sliver of light from the kitchen lit the darkened room. My hand still gripped our cordless phone.

"Hey," I whispered to Larry. He was already in bed but fluffed up a pillow, stuck it behind his back, and sat up against it.

"What did they say?" he asked. He moved the sheet and blanket to make space for me at the edge of the bed. I told him what I could remember and then shared what I'd been asked.

"They want to know when they can expect me," I said.

His eyes met mine, and he took my hand. He knew how big of an ask that was.

Larry and I had been together for more than a decade, and he well knew my history—and my heart—when it came to my dad. We'd lived our lives without a word from him for seven years. We hardly spoke of him anymore. But more than knowing what the past decade had been like for me living estranged from my dad, he knew what I'd been through as a child and how everything had fallen apart, over and over again.

Larry had also been there for me as I'd learned to heal from those childhood wounds, as I'd learned to look at relationships and myself differently, as I'd learned to move on. To forgive. To try to forget.

I'd worked hard to move forward. My fear in going to Wisconsin was that I'd be taking giant steps back. And into what? Would my dad be conscious and live through this? Or would he die?

"They're expecting someone to go," I said quietly.

Larry didn't say a word. He just rubbed his thumb along mine and looked at me sympathetically.

"It's like someone held open my position even though I'd told them I wasn't coming back," I blurted out.

If I were to go back, I feared I would get caught up in what it meant. Would our relationship finally change? Would I expect him to become the father I'd always wanted him to be? I knew that wouldn't happen.

"I can't go." I got up and began to pace the room.

Larry cocked his head in response but said nothing.

"Who would take care of the kids?" I turned to look at him. "We both just started new jobs."

It was impossible. Impractical. Imposing.

"We can't afford a plane ticket," I went on, searching for more excuses. "And I'd have to pay for a hotel room too. We can't do it. We're already in debt."

"Uh huh," Larry offered, though I knew none of that mattered to him as much as my peace of mind. He'd support me, whatever I wanted to do.

"It's two weeks before Christmas, for God's sake!" I continued. "We need to buy presents and decorate the tree and . . ."

How could my dad do this to me? is what I really wanted to say. Was it reasonable to be angry with him even though he lay unresponsive in a hospital bed and certainly hadn't planned for this to happen? I stopped pacing and looked at the phone in my hand.

"Are you going to call the nurse back?" Larry asked.

"No," I said defiantly. "I'm going to call my mom."

If ever there was a time I needed to hear her voice, it was now, and she needed to know what had happened. She'd once cared about my dad and had loved him as fiercely as I had. She'd also understand why I just couldn't go. Why I didn't want to. I punched in her cell number and waited for her to pick up.

There was no answer and no option to leave a message.

I tried again. And again.

I punched her number in five times before I remembered that she and Charlie were on vacation in Georgia, and she'd told me they wouldn't have cell service. I bore my eyes into the phone—disbelieving and desperate to talk with her. What was I supposed to do?

"She's out of range." I plopped down on the bed again next to Larry. "I forgot she's on vacation."

The phone weighed heavy in my hand.

What was I going to tell the nurse?

I didn't know any friends my dad might have or anyone who'd be willing to go to Milwaukee to be there for him. My Aunt Eunice, though she still had a soft spot for him and let him come by once in a while, was in her seventies with failing health. She wouldn't be driving to the big city.

"Who will go if I don't?" I whispered in the dark.

Larry reached for my hand. He knew what I knew.

No one.

CHAPTER 6
The Sky was Crying

JANUARY 1981

At the age of thirteen I learned that nothing is for keeps. Not even brothers.

The year started off with brownie baking at Grandma's, bowling with my dad, and a party for Cliff's third birthday. Each weekend I spent with Dad, Cliff, Clint, and Grandma, which was nearly every weekend, was the best. I know because I'd started keeping a diary again, and I'd graded all those days A+.

I decorated Cliff's birthday cake myself. Dad bought toy guitars for both Cliff and Clint and restrung the acoustic one he'd bought me for my tenth birthday. I started playing in my youth-group band at church. Dad was playing again, too, and was back to singing his favorite songs.

Our time together that spring and summer was filled with fun. Birthday parties, graduations, and weddings for our many cousins. Lazy afternoons at the lake, grilling out and playing frisbee. We played cards, went out for pizza, and I even got to shoot my dad's BB gun.

Dad and I didn't talk about Debra. He didn't tell me what finally ended their relationship, and I didn't care. I was just happy it was over. No more tension. No more stress. Since Cliff and Clint were picked up before I was every weekend, I never even saw Debra. But on a drizzly Saturday in September, almost a year after their divorce, I learned she could still wreak havoc in my life.

Despite the dreary weather, I'd been looking forward to another weekend together. I hoped I'd get to play cards with Grandma for a bit while Dad hung out with the boys. Then maybe we'd make ice-cream sundaes, and when the skies cleared, I'd take the boys out puddle jumping.

I watched the raindrops stream down our front window as I waited for my dad to pick me up that afternoon. As soon as I saw his clunky car round the corner onto our street, I hollered goodbye to my mom and Charlie and headed out to the curb. My dad never parked in our driveway or walked up to our front door, even when the weather was fine.

Covering my head with my hoodie, I ran to his car. The cold, hard drops pelted me. I plopped into the front passenger seat, threw back my hood, and turned around to say hello to the boys, but all I found was empty space.

"Where are Cliff and Clint?" I asked. They hadn't joined us for a few weeks, but I hadn't questioned their absence. I thought maybe Debra had taken them on vacation.

My dad stared through his fogged-up windshield. Heat radiated from the front vents.

"In a minute," he said, his eyes searching for the road, his hands holding tight to the steering wheel. We were out of my neighborhood before he spoke again.

"So?" I asked.

"Debra's getting married," he said.

I shrugged. What did that have to do with anything? I

threw my overnight bag behind me, onto the empty back seats.

"So, the boys," he began, staring straight ahead. He took a moment and then told me that they wouldn't be coming. Not that day or any day in the future. They'd never be coming again.

"What?" This made no sense.

"Debra wants her new husband to adopt them," he said. "We can't see them anymore."

"What?" I almost laughed out loud. "Well, that's stupid. She can't do that." I held the sleeves of my wet sweatshirt up to the heater vents.

My dad was silent. And the intense look on his face worried me.

"Can she?" I wasn't laughing now.

He didn't look my way.

"Why would she do that?" Fear gripped me at the thought of this being possible. "You're not gonna let her do that . . ."

He took a breath, exhaled, and softly—without looking my direction—said, "I have to."

I shook my head. "You have to?"

I waited.

"*You have to?*" I asked again, louder this time. "You're their *dad!* What do you mean you *have* to?"

I wanted him to stop the car. To pull over. To face me.

He stayed on the road, driving through the downpour that now felt so appropriate. The sky was crying. My heart was breaking. How could he just keep going?

"I don't want to, but I have to," he said finally, his voice little more than a whisper. His hands shook on the wheel. I studied his face. Watched him hold back his tears.

He couldn't afford to keep them, he explained. Couldn't pay the child support.

It was hard to find work, he said. He was doing all he could, he said.

"Debra said if I can't pay, I can't see them. I have to let them go, Bessers. I have no choice."

I didn't know what to say. I pictured Cliff, rough and tumble at three, running around the house and playing peek-a-boo. I saw Clint, just two, laying his head on my shoulder and falling asleep in my arms.

"Can *I* see them?" I asked.

We were a block or two from Grandma's house. He pulled the car over to the side of the road, and finally shut it off. He looked my way, closed his eyes, and shook his head. No.

There were no words.

"I'm so sorry," he said. A single tear fell down his cheek. "We can't see them until they're eighteen."

"Eighteen?" I raised my voice in disbelief and anger at the injustice of it all. "But I haven't done anything wrong! You divorced her, not me! Why can't *I* see them?"

"I'm giving up my rights to them, Bessers, and if I can't have anything to do with them, neither can you."

Don't call me Bessers right now! I wanted to shout. It didn't soften the blow.

"Anyway," he added, "they've moved."

My heart cracked wide open.

I turned away and pressed my forehead against the freezing window.

We continued to Grandma's in silence.

How was it possible that I'd never again get to tuck my baby brothers into bed or kiss their little heads goodnight? I'd never again get to hug them or hear them giggle. How could they just be gone? Just be taken from me? I hadn't even had a chance to say goodbye.

My dad parked on Eighth Street in front of Grandma's house. *Does she already know?*

What would Cliff and Clint be told?

Would they really be eighteen before we'd see them again?

The last time I'd seen them had been the fifth of July. I'd written in my diary that we'd played frisbee, ate fried chicken, and Dad had told jokes all day. I hadn't known it was the last time we'd be together.

I've lost my brothers.

It was unbelievable. It was wrong. But it was happening.

I grabbed my overnight bag from the back seat, avoided my dad's gaze, and stepped out of the car and into a world without Cliff and Clint.

I've lost— I kept repeating, though I couldn't make myself believe it *—my brothers.*

I stomped up the seven steps to the porch landing and was reaching for the door handle when a switch flipped in my head.

I am NOT losing my brothers, my inner voice boomed.

So what if my dad can't afford to keep them. So what if Debra has them now and her stupid new husband might adopt them.

I'm their big sister and I. Am. Never. Letting. Go.

I opened the door and walked in with a confidence I could not explain.

CHAPTER 7
I Wish You Well

DECEMBER 1981

No one knew of the plan I'd concocted to reach out to Cliff and Clint. No one needed to. I decided that at thirteen I was old enough to make this decision on my own. I was also afraid that if anyone knew, they would try to stop me. So, I told no one and chose a strategic time to make the phone call I'd hoped would connect me to my brothers.

Though I'd thought of them often—with renewed anger bubbling up each time at the injustice of being separated from them—the days leading up to the holidays had been especially hard. While I'd vowed to myself that I'd stay connected to them, I hadn't been able to think of a way to do it. Had they left the city? Left the state? I had no idea how to find them. But it was Christmastime. I had to!

Then I remembered someone who might help me. An ally who loved the boys as much as I did and who would want the best for them. I couldn't believe I hadn't thought of her sooner.

I'd met her just a few weeks after meeting Debra, soon after moving back to Sheboygan. Debra's mother and father still lived in the farmhouse Debra had grown up in on the outskirts of town, and I was surprised by Debra's invitation one weekend to go meet them. I was even more surprised by our mode of transportation: Debra's motorcycle.

"Let's ride to my house," she'd said one morning shortly after I'd arrived. Within minutes, she'd mounted her Harley and was handing me a helmet. These were the early days when I was in awe of her. I was nine, and the motorcycle ride would be my first.

I swung my leg over the back of the seat, pulled the helmet over my head, and did my best to steady myself as we started down the road. I felt so grown up and honored that she would take me home to meet her parents.

Debra smiled from behind the dark shield of her own helmet looking at our reflection in her rearview mirror. I smiled back. It was a perfect day. Brilliant blue and not a cloud in the sky.

"Hang on tight!" she said over her shoulder, and she hit the gas. I tried.

My helmet was loose, and my arms didn't reach all the way around her black leather jacket, but I pushed my fears away. We raced down the open roads past rows of cornfields and grazing cows. A feeling of absolute freedom shot through me.

Gravel spit out from under the tires as we made our way up her parents' long driveway. Debra's childhood home was classic Wisconsin. Quaint and cozy, with a white fence around the perimeter; a big, red barn; and a silver silo.

Her father tended the land and was out on his tractor when we arrived. Her mother, Rose, was scattering chicken feed near the henhouse. After giving me a warm hug hello, she led us into their kitchen to have a snack—chocolate chip cookies fresh out of the oven.

She poured me a glass of milk, handed me the daintiest China plate with two cookies on it, and motioned for me to have a seat at the table. I looked out through her kitchen window as she and Debra made small talk. There were more rows of corn, and more cows, cats, and ducks, than I could count. I felt giddy with delight.

Thinking back on that day after I'd come to know Debra better, I couldn't help but see the vast contrast between her and her mother. To me, Debra was black and white, like the photos she'd developed the day she'd taken me to the darkroom at her junior college. Black hair, leather jacket, black boots. Snow White skin. Ivory soap. The pantry door that the spaghetti slid down.

Rose was like a palette of watercolors. Soft yellow like the sun's rays that streamed through her kitchen window. Light green like the leaves on the corn stalks outside. Pale blue like the color of the sky in her eyes.

That evening, I asked Debra for her parents' address and phone number, and carefully printed the information in my pink, flowered address book. I'd catalogued all the people who were important to me since second grade. I visited the farmhouse only a few times after that, and I'd never had a need to call, but four years later during the week before Christmas when I was missing my brothers the most, I remembered that I had it.

Alone in my bedroom that December night, I opened my address book and found the page it was written on. How perfect that I'd had this revelation at Christmastime! Rose would be so happy to hear from me. But before I called, I needed to make sure the coast was clear.

We had three phones in our house, and the one with the longest cord was on the hallway wall right across from my bedroom. I slid open my pocket door and peeked out to check on the status of the household. Brett, now six, was fast asleep in his bedroom just next to mine on the third floor. My mom and Charlie were two floors below, in our family room watching *The Love Boat*.

As quietly as I could, I tiptoed across the hall, removed the phone receiver from its cradle, and stretched its mustard-colored spiral cord toward my room and under my sliding door. I took a deep breath, hoping for the best, and punched the buttons. It had been at least six months since I'd last seen Rose. *Did she even know I wasn't allowed to see my brothers?*

One ring. Then two. Until her sweet voice said hello.

I pictured her answering the phone in her kitchen, where I'd sat four long years earlier enjoying my milk and cookies, feeling content with the world. Before everything changed. Before the fighting. Before the divorce. Before the boys went away. I pictured the farmland that stretched far beyond the house, and her blue eyes, her gentle smile.

She was surprised to hear from me—I hadn't been given the opportunity to say goodbye to her either—but she welcomed my call.

I can do this. I thought of my plan and just knew she was going to help me.

I got right to the point, my Christmas wish.

"I know I can't see Cliff and Clint this Christmas, but I'd like to send them presents." I paused to give her a moment. "Would that be okay?"

I held my breath as I waited for her to say *Yes, of course! What a wonderful idea!* But her response took longer than I thought it would, and the change in her voice when she replied took me by surprise.

"Um." She hesitated. "Debra wouldn't like that."

I was dumbfounded. Shocked. She was my ally. Surely, she of all people could see how wrong this situation was.

"But I just want to send them gifts," I said. Maybe she'd misunderstood. "I don't have to see them."

My words were met with silence. "I just want them to know I'm thinking of them." *Help me here!*

I waited again, hoping she was working out a plan. We didn't have to tell Debra. *Please.*

"It's probably best if you don't call here anymore," she said softly, and in the nicest possible way. "I wish you well, dear." Then she was gone.

I sat on my bed, mouth open, staring at the receiver in my hand.

That was it? That was the end? Not only could I not see them, I couldn't even let them know I was thinking of them. Even at Christmastime.

I'd thought I was so clever, that my plan would work for sure. Now I'd lost them and Rose, too.

How I wished I could run and hug my mom and tell her what had happened. I needed for her to tell me everything was going to be okay. She'd help me find a way to stay connected. But how could she help now? I'd burned my only bridge.

I crawled under the covers of my bed and cried until my nose was so stuffy I could barely breathe and my stomach muscles ached. I thought of how I'd stomped up Grandma's steps a few months back, so determined to hang onto my brothers, so confident that I could.

Now I knew I was powerless. I had no choice but to let go.

CHAPTER 8
Ray of Sunshine

JANUARY 1982

I hoped the new year would bring me happiness though I wasn't sure how that could happen. I certainly didn't expect it to come in the form of my dad's new girlfriend. He'd met Sherry over the holidays—the holidays we had spent without Cliff and Clint—and the three of us celebrated her twenty-second birthday a week after I'd met her. My dad was thirty-seven. I would turn fourteen that April and complete ninth grade that spring.

I melted in her warmth. Her poofy blond hair bounced around on her head when she laughed, which was often, and her bright blue eyes lit up behind the thick lenses of her glasses when she told stories. She hugged me and made me feel included. Sherry was a ray of sunshine in my life.

In fact, Sherry was from a whole family of warm, wonderful people. Her parents, two sisters, and three brothers all lived in Sheboygan, and many of my weekends with my dad, who seemed happy once again, were spent with all of them. Family gatherings were often in Sherry's parents' basement bar where drinks flowed and laughter reigned. I hung out with her younger sister who was a senior in high school, and I looked forward to spending time not only with my dad and Sherry, but with her whole family who had taken me in like one of their own.

"We're going to get married in May," Sherry shared with me one Sunday afternoon in March. Despite the short time she'd been in our lives, I knew Sherry was just what my dad and I needed. I was ecstatic!

"And we're going to have a baby."

That was more surprising, but I was thrilled at the idea of Sherry and her family having a permanent place in my life and at the thought of having another half-brother or a half-sister to love. I didn't think about the age difference between my dad and Sherry. I didn't think about the financial responsibility of him having another child. I was happy for him. He'd made a fresh start, and everything was going to be okay again.

After being dropped off at our curb that evening, I strode up the driveway to my house with a skip in my step, humming a favorite tune my dad had taught me. Something about a silly, old ant who thought he could move a rubber-tree plant because he had high hopes. High-in-the-sky-apple-pie-hopes! I knew just how he felt.

I announced my news as soon as I got in our front door. My mom and Charlie just happened to be passing through the foyer the moment I came in.

"Isn't it great?" I threw my arms up in the air for emphasis and smiled my widest smile. My mom's forehead crinkled. She looked from me to Charlie, who just shook his head back and forth.

Feeling irritated with them and alone in my joy, I flew past them and ran upstairs with the excuse of wanting to take my overnight bag to my room. I couldn't stand looking at their condescending faces. Why couldn't they just be happy for him, for God's sake?

"Take a shower, honey" my mom yelled up the stairs behind me. "You smell like an ashtray."

It was true. I did. And I didn't like it either. But she didn't have to say it.

I smelled like Grandma's house, and I loved Grandma's house. Even though its walls were permanently tinted brown from three generations of smokers in our family, including Grandma and my dad, and even though by the time I left there I smelled like I'd smoked a pack myself. It was one of my favorite places on Earth, and I didn't want to be told to wash off the stench of it when I got home.

I also didn't want to hear my mom's and Charlie's opinions of my dad and Sherry. Their faces had said enough, and it hadn't been the first time they'd rolled their eyes at one of his decisions. Though sometimes my mom and Charlie turned out to be right, this time I knew they were dead wrong. Sherry was the best thing that had ever happened to my dad.

At dinner a few weeks later, Charlie dropped a bomb. Someone had made an anonymous call to Sherry's father regarding my dad.

"They said Sherry shouldn't marry him," Charlie said.

I stopped chewing my bite of broccoli. *What?*

Who would do that? And why shouldn't Sherry marry my dad?

"Really?" my mom asked. I couldn't read the emotion on her face. Was she as shocked as I was, or had Charlie already told her?

"Why?" I snapped, startling Brett. He looked up from his plate.

Charlie stopped eating and rested his fork on the table. I

lowered my eyes, hoping not to get in trouble for my outburst, no longer hungry.

"Well," Charlie went on, "they said she's too young for Roy."

Hearing my dad's name on Charlie's lips made me queasy.

"I mean, there are more than fifteen years between them. Heck, she's hardly older than you, right?" He gestured my way.

My skin prickled.

"Anyway, they told her dad that Roy's been married twice already and gave up two kids for adoption."

So what? She should just leave my dad? We'd already lost Cliff and Clint. I couldn't imagine us losing Sherry too.

"They were just thinking of Sherry's best interests." Charlie stabbed a piece of pork chop with his fork. He may as well have been stabbing my heart.

Why was he telling me all of this? Was he trying to ruin my happiness? Glad that someone was trying to ruin my dad's? I knew he didn't think much of him, and he didn't understand why I did.

"Who told you all this?" I asked him, trying not to be "emotional," as he'd often accused me of being.

Charlie reached for his drink. "Debra called here earlier."

"What?" The mention of her name triggered me. Did she have something to do with this? Hadn't she done enough damage?

"Your dad called her. He was pretty upset. He thought maybe her husband had called Sherry's dad."

Of course my dad was upset! I wanted to shout.

"*Was* it him?"

"No, it wasn't him." Charlie cut off another bite of his pork chop, slowly put it in his mouth and chewed.

"Then who—" I stopped when I saw the answer shining in his eyes. He'd wanted me to see it.

My hands hit the table, alarming my mom and Brett. I

pushed back my chair and sprang to my feet. I'd always been so careful to not make a scene. Not overreact or raise my voice. But this time, I was unwilling, and I didn't care what the repercussions might be.

"They love each other!" I yelled. "And this is going to work out!"

The three of them stared at me wide-eyed.

"They're going to get married and have a baby and stay together. You'll see!" I headed out of the kitchen but turned back once more. "Why can't you just be happy for him?"

I ran through the living room and up the stairs to my room, stopping only to slam my door shut before crashing into my bed and sobbing.

Any moment, I expected to hear Charlie's footsteps on the stairs. He'd knock at my door and then come in uninvited to tell me what I'd done was unacceptable. He would ground me for sure. He'd done it for far less.

Silence enveloped me. And shockingly, that's all there was for the rest of the evening. No consequence. No retaliation. Perhaps because Charlie had been the instigator, he'd decided to let it go.

A couple months later, despite his interference and to my sheer delight, my dad and Sherry got married, and my half-sister, Tara, was born in October. When I visited on the weekends, sometimes we'd hang out with Sherry's big, loud, lovable family, and sometimes it would be just the four of us. I loved our new, smaller family too.

My dad was back to joking and singing and enjoying life. Sherry was like a big sister to me, and I loved spending time with her and Tara. Looking into my baby sister's face reminded me of my brothers, of course, and I still held out hope for a future that included them. I didn't know how I'd make it happen, but I wouldn't be helpless forever.

That Christmas, Tara's first, was magical. Sherry's parents

threw a huge holiday bash in their basement bar, and we drank eggnog, played pool, sang carols, and even got a visit from Santa. I was so excited to celebrate with all of them, blissfully unaware that life with my dad, Sherry, and Tara would ever be anything but happy.

Part Two

CHAPTER 9
The Crack in His Voice

DECEMBER 1983

For Tara's second Christmas, there would again be a big holiday party at Sherry's parents' house on Christmas Day. Once again, Santa would visit. But I wouldn't be there. I would see my dad, Sherry, and Tara the day after Christmas, and we would celebrate then.

It was disappointing to know I'd miss being with Sherry's whole family, but I was also looking forward to spending Christmas Eve and Christmas Day the way I always had, with my mom, Charlie, and Brett. We would go to church on Christmas Eve, have dinner afterward at Charlie's parents' house with his sisters and brothers and their children, and come home to find that Santa had delivered our presents. Our tradition was to open them on Christmas Eve because on Christmas morning, we would travel to Manitowoc to celebrate with my mom's family.

I'd joyfully marked off each day of December on my Mary Engelbreit calendar. I was looking forward to all of it but especially excited about giving my dad the gift I'd made for him that year.

My friend Peggy had inspired me to do something creative. The previous Christmas, she'd given me a special gift, a large, rectangular glass jar, like one you find in a craft store, that she had découpaged with brightly colored cutouts from magazines. Each side of the jar was plastered with phrases that reflected on our five years of friendship, from the ages of five to fifteen. Statements she'd chosen, like "I Never Go Alone" and "Built to Last," reminded me of how strong our bond was. Names of favorite places we'd been together, like Marriott's Great America, and clips like "Hall & Oates" reminded me of great memories we shared. On top of the jar's wooden lid, Peggy had pasted a cutout that read, "From someone who loves you, a gift to hold the things you love."

Every time I looked at her gift, it made me smile. I wanted to put that kind of smile on my dad's face.

I spent hours scouring the pages of my mom's *Good Housekeeping* and *Reader's Digest* and Charlie's *Consumer Reports* and *Money* magazines to find just the right words and phrases that would express my love for him and remind him of our favorite things. I carefully pasted everything in just the right place on a large jar I'd bought with my babysitting money, then took great care to découpage it. I was thrilled with the results and gleefully wrapped up the gift, along with the gifts I'd bought for Sherry, Tara, and Grandma, and placed them near the back of our Christmas tree in the living room.

The day after Christmas, as I was putting a few last-minute items into my suitcase, the phone rang. I picked up the receiver outside my bedroom door.

"Hello?" I answered, barely able to contain my excitement. I hoped it was my dad saying he would soon be on his way.

"Hi, Bessers," he said. Excitement flooded through me. I pictured him on the other end being just as excited as I was.

I stretched the long, coiled phone cord into my room to finish packing while we talked.

"Are you leaving now?" I cradled the phone between my ear and shoulder so I could use both hands to zip my suitcase. My dad and I lived just twenty minutes apart, so I knew it wouldn't be long before he arrived. It took me a second to register his silence.

"Um, no," he said.

I took the receiver back in my hand and pressed it to my ear.

"Well," I tried to hide my impatience. "When *are* you leaving?"

More silence.

"I can't . . ." he began. "I can't come today."

He paused, and I held my breath.

"I'll come . . . in a few days," he said. "The twenty-ninth, okay?"

I tried to sound cheerful in my response. No big deal. Surely there was a good reason why he couldn't come that day. I tempered my disappointment and looked forward to seeing him in three days.

I pulled his jar and the presents for Sherry, Tara, and Grandma from under the tree and put them in a corner of my room where they stayed while those three days crawled by.

On the afternoon of the twenty-ninth, I passed by the grandfather clock in our living room just before two o'clock, my dad's planned time of arrival. I moved the gifts and my suitcase to the foyer, put my winter coat on, and waited for him. Through the vertical window next to our front door, I watched cars intermittently drive down our not-so-busy street, leaving their dirty tire tracks in the freshly fallen snow. My dad's car was not one of them.

Twenty minutes. I took off my coat and hung it up on the rack nearby.

Forty minutes. I stared at his usual parking spot, by the curb next to our mailbox, and willed him to arrive.

Then I heard the phone ring.

I ran down the front hall to our kitchen and grabbed the receiver from the phone on the wall.

"Hello?"

"Hi, Bessers." It was my dad, but the crack in his voice caught me off-guard.

"Hi!" I was relieved to hear his voice despite being disappointed that he was late. "Will you be here soon?"

If he was calling from Grandma's, I knew he would be.

"No," he said.

I sucked in a breath, annoyed. Then fearful that he might postpone again.

"Well, what time *will* you be here?" I twisted the mustard-colored phone cord around my finger. "When are you coming?"

"I'm not." He paused. "I can't make it today."

Tears welled in my eyes. "Well, when can you make it?" I said it so sweetly, holding all my hurt inside.

"I'm not going to be able to make it at all," he said. His voice was flat, revealing nothing. "I can't talk about it right now."

I pressed my lips together and didn't make a sound.

I'm sure there's a reason, I said to myself over and over, just as I had so many times before when I'd tried to justify my dad's seemingly unexplainable actions.

"I've gotta go," he said softly. "I'm sorry. I'll call you soon." He paused again. "Merry Christmas, Bessers."

"Merry Chris——," I began, my voice barely audible. And the line went dead.

CHAPTER 10
No Boats Today

JANUARY 1984

In the Wisconsin winters of my childhood, snow started falling weeks before Thanksgiving and sometimes didn't stop until Easter. Those wondrous flakes would blanket my world in white, making everything sparkle for a while, before they were plowed and shoveled and stomped on. Before they turned to grimy, gray slush and became slick sheets of ice. During Wisconsin winters, everything repeatedly froze, thawed, and froze again.

In the months after my dad canceled Christmas, the same could have been said of my heart, which melted at the thought of missing him but hardened again each day that went by without a word.

January passed without a whisper. There were no weekends at my dad's. No word from him. No Sherry. No Tara. No Grandma.

Valentine's Day brought no card, no candy, no call. I wondered if I'd done something to make him stay away, or if he'd forgotten me altogether.

St. Patrick's Day came and went. I wanted to call him but felt I couldn't. I shouldn't. It seemed intrusive. *Besides,* I thought, *he's the parent, he should call me.*

And then he did.

"Hey, Bessers! Happy Birthday!" he said when I answered the phone. It was the seventh of April, my sixteenth birthday. There was a lilt in his voice, as if everything was normal. I prickled at the sound of my nickname rolling so easily off his tongue after so much time apart.

"Can I see you this weekend?" he asked as if it were nothing.

I had dared to hope he'd call—and he'd even called on my actual birthday—but how could he just move on with no apology, no explanation? He'd been twenty minutes away for more than three months!

"I'm busy this weekend," I told him, which was true, but it felt good to deny him, even if just for a moment. "Next weekend's okay though," I found myself saying. I couldn't keep the ice from melting.

We made plans for the following Sunday, and I prayed he'd show up. I spent the week vacillating between feeling excited about seeing him, Sherry, Tara, and Grandma, and feeling sad that I'd missed Christmas with them. I was relieved to know he still cared but was angry about the months that had gone by.

I didn't pack a suitcase for this visit. I didn't want to spend the night.

I brought no gifts. My dad's jar sat in my closet, along with the gifts for Sherry, Tara, and Grandma. Maybe I would rewrap them for their birthdays. Sherry's had already passed in January, but Grandma's and Tara's would be that fall. How embarrassing it would have been to give them out that April, a clear reminder that they'd celebrated without me, that I was separate. I didn't know if I'd ever give the jar to my dad. Its pasted-on messages were full of love and reminders of happy moments. None of that seemed to matter anymore.

My dad, upon arrival at my house, seemed unfazed by the passing of so much time, greeting me by my nickname and reaching over to hug me after I climbed into his car. I leaned in and let him, but I didn't hug back. I hadn't been sure how I'd feel once I saw him. Now I did. I felt numb, guarded, sad.

"How are you?" he said, all smiles. "How's it feel to be sixteen?"

He reached for my left knee—for a particular spot he'd discovered when I was little—that tickled and typically sent me into a fit of giggles. But not that day. That day it just felt weird to have his hand on my knee.

"I'm fine," I lied, and moved my knees toward the passenger door, out of his reach. I stared out the front window.

He shrugged and put his hand back on the steering wheel. I expected him to try the next sure thing to make me laugh—driving with no hands.

"How are you doing that?" I'd ask in amazement as he drove down the road with both hands in the air. As I grew older and realized he was using his knees, it became a silly thing we joked about.

His eyes flashed in the direction of my face, and I could feel my heart beginning to thaw—from his touch, from the way he'd smiled at me, from the love that shone through his eyes, even if only in a glance. Conflicting emotions ebbed and flowed like waves beneath my skin. I didn't want to feel sad or angry but being happy too soon would wash away my pain too quickly, before he faced it, before he acknowledged it. Half of me wanted to make him feel as terrible as he'd made me feel, but the other half wanted to hug him and never let go. I wanted to share everything on my mind but was afraid that if I did, I would lose him again. So I said nothing at all.

"We're going to Grandma's," he said, breaking the silence.

"Okay," I said, staring out the passenger-side window as if I didn't care. Then I wondered why we'd be going to Grandma's house instead of his. Would Sherry and Tara be there?

He took our usual route down North Avenue, past McDonald's, my high school, and the Starlite bowling alley, and then circled the roundabout that led to the south side. No jokes. No attempt at conversation.

As we approached the Eighth Street Bridge, I pressed my forehead against the window and scanned the Sheboygan River below. It was a habit from childhood to seek out boats that looked too tall to fit under the drawbridge. A too-tall boat meant the bridge would have to open. It was one of my favorite things about a trip to Grandma's house. We always took the same route, so the possibility was always there.

The opening of the bridge was a big production. Bells would clang, traffic would stop, and cherry-red lights would flash wildly from black-and-white crossing signs, like at a railroad track. The massive steel bridge before us would crack open in the middle and slowly rise on each side. One half would face away from us, toward Grandma's house a block away. The other half would come up in front of us, like a great wall, right before our very eyes. No matter how many times we saw it, my dad and I would both stare, transfixed, as the whole process played out.

"I loved this when I was a kid!" my dad would say every time.

"I love it, too," I'd tell him. And neither of us needed to say anything more.

As a child, I'd crossed my fingers each time we'd approached, hoping for a show, but on that April day—a week after my sixteenth birthday and more than three months after my worst Christmas ever—I just wanted to get to Grandma's.

"No boats today," my dad said. He had scanned the river too.

"No." I stole a glance in his direction.

I loved him so much.

We crossed the bridge, both of us no doubt remembering happier times but neither of us saying a word.

We were just a few minutes from Grandma's, which settled my nerves. Seeing her, seeing Sherry and Tara, would make things better again. I turned around to see the bridge through the back window and watched until it disappeared from my view. My eyes fell to my dad's back seat where unopened mail was strewn. Crumpled McDonald's and Hardee's bags and empty cans of Pepsi lay on the floorboard. Poking out from under them was a crushed carton of Viceroy cigarettes. My dad turned to me as if to say something but stopped short. He pulled up against the curb in front of Grandma's house and parked.

Despite feeling out of place in my dad's life at that moment, it was comforting to be back on Eighth Street. At least at Grandma's, I knew what to expect. Sugared orange slices in a crystal bowl on the living room table. Grandma in the kitchen listening to her police scanner. A stack of cards waiting for us to play Rummy 500. Many things had changed, but some things never would, I was sure.

Grandma was in the kitchen when I arrived. I rushed past the sugared orange slices and into her arms to hug her tight. She wished me a happy birthday, kissed my cheek, and adjusted the elastic waistband of her brown polyester pants before sitting down at the kitchen table. The cards were out. I sat down next to her.

Dad came in and eyed the hamburgers she'd been cooking on the stove. They were almost ready.

"Why don't we open your birthday presents before we eat?" she suggested.

Oh, okay . . . I see. We're just gonna pretend the last few months didn't happen.

Though I would have liked some explanation, I was actually relieved. We were just going to move forward, and I was fine with that.

"The presents are in the back room, Ma," my dad chimed in, but he didn't move to get them. I pushed my chair out from the table and headed there, saving Grandma from getting up.

"Your Christmas presents are back there, too," he said, now following behind me. "I'll help you bring them out."

The word Christmas stopped me in my tracks.

I thought we were going to forget about all that . . .

My dad moved past me, getting to the room first. I stood still, trying to keep my head together.

Do not say a word.

I walked slowly on the yellowed squares of Grandma's linoleum floor to where they met the gray, threadbare carpet of the back room. I was barely through the narrow door frame when I felt the tears coming.

Do not cry.

Maybe giving me the Christmas presents was my dad's way of saying he was sorry he'd missed it. I imagined him saying, "Let's forget all about that nonsense and just be happy again. We're together now. I love you."

But he didn't say anything. He just scooped up a few small gifts wrapped in red paper and punctuated with silver bows and went back to the kitchen. I heard him behind me, setting them up on the table.

I stood in the drafty room looking at the last two gifts, the ones he'd left for me to carry. One was wrapped in red like the ones he'd taken. The other was wrapped in pink. I picked up the pink one, my birthday present, I presumed, and carried it to the kitchen table. I wasn't about to pick up my own Christmas present—from a Christmas we didn't celebrate together—and bring it to the table. I didn't want any of those Christmas gifts anyway. They would only remind me of everything I'd been trying to forget.

"Hey," I said, finally settling in at the table, "where are Sherry and Tara?" No one had even mentioned them. "Are we going to your house later?" I looked at my dad. His eyes met Grandma's.

"Are they coming here?" I started ripping off pink wrapping paper.

"Bessers . . ." my dad began. I cringed again at hearing him call me by that name, but his hesitation caught my attention. I stopped unwrapping.

"Bessers . . ." he started again, more softly this time, and the blood drained away from his face. He looked down. I stared at the top of his head and then looked into Grandma's eyes, trying to register what they weren't saying.

"What is it?" I asked, but my brain was already connecting the dots: our canceled Christmas, three months of silence, his awkwardness on the drive over, the mess in his backseat, the absence of Sherry and Tara at Grandma's house.

Suddenly, I knew. I knew, but I didn't want to let my mind think it. I didn't want to believe it was true.

More than two years had passed since we'd lost Cliff and Clint. I was older now. Wiser. I knew my dad was capable of doing things beyond my comprehension. But I couldn't believe he'd done it again. Sherry and Tara were already gone, and again, I hadn't even been given a chance to say goodbye.

Grandma opened her arms to me, her eyes wet with sadness, and I fell into her.

CHAPTER 11
The Middle of the Mess

DECEMBER 9, 2003

I pictured my dad lying alone on his bed in an intensive care room at Froedtert Hospital in Milwaukee, eleven hundred miles from where I sat on mine, holding Larry's hand in the darkness.

If I didn't go to Froedtert, my dad would continue to lie there alone. If worse came to worst, he would die there alone. I couldn't bear the thought of it.

But if I decided to go, I would go for him. Because he needed me. As for myself, I was done needing him.

Or was I?

I'd buried my desire to care.

But maybe—

Just maybe, I needed to see him. Maybe this was the way that things were supposed to happen. Maybe even though I didn't want to go, didn't believe I should have to go, maybe it was where I physically needed to be. Right there in the middle of the mess—amid the chaos that had ensued and the chaos that might come of it.

Either way, I'd finally get an ending to our story. Should he live, I'd get to say goodbye on my own terms and not expect anything more from him. Should he die, I'd get to say goodbye before he was gone forever. I would no longer live in expectation or wonder. I'd no longer wait for reconnection. I'd walk away knowing it would never come.

If I went, my visit would be our last.

I imagined him there, his head on a white pillow, a white sheet tucked around him, his eyes closed. Just waiting.

"No one else will go." The thought escaped my lips as a whisper. The phone receiver was still clutched in my hand. Nurse Sally was waiting for me to call back.

My dad, no matter what kind of dad he'd been, was still a human being, and he deserved better than having nobody by his side. I couldn't let that happen, as if he mattered to no one. He had once mattered so very much to me.

I gripped Larry's hand and looked at the receiver. Larry squeezed back.

"You should go," he said softly. And I knew that I would.

I called Nurse Sally at Froedtert shortly after ten o'clock that night.

"Thursday," I told her. "I'll be there around noon."

I'd charged a round-trip ticket to Milwaukee, putting us nearly five-hundred dollars further in debt, but at least I'd been able to find a flight leaving Tallahassee at eight o'clock Thursday morning so I wouldn't have to pay weekend fare. Another seventy dollars went on our MasterCard to pay for a room at a Holiday Inn near the hospital where I would stay Thursday night.

My return flight would leave just after two o'clock Friday afternoon, giving me twenty-four hours to take care of things as next of kin—talk with the doctors, fill out paperwork, and of course, see my dad. I didn't think any more time would be necessary, and since I couldn't afford to stay longer anyway, I wasn't concerned about the time constraint. I'd be there and back by the end of the week, having fulfilled my obligations—and settled my heart.

"I'll schedule a time for you to meet with the staff," Nurse Sally told me.

"All right," I said, ready to move forward.

"Will anyone else be coming with you?"

She couldn't see my mouth drop. I had already figured out so much. *Sally, there is no one else*, was all I could think, but I didn't say it out loud.

"Well," she continued after my lack of response. "Your father's been transferred to our trauma room. He's intubated. Before you come, you'll want to think about your family's wishes."

Our family's wishes—what a strange thing to hear.

He'd had children, yes, but we weren't a family. We were bits and pieces spread out in separate cities and states, leading separate lives. We had three different mothers and five stepfathers between us. And we each had lived most of our lives without our "dad."

He doesn't have a family to make those wishes, I wanted to tell her, but then my mind went back to the last day I'd seen him, that October day in 1996 when Larry and I had visited him in Sheboygan.

"Oh, I have something to show you," he'd said near the end of our time together, and from under an end table in his living room, he'd pulled out a large photo album, the kind with beige boards and sticky cellophane flaps. Stuck to the first several pages were photographs of me, Cliff, Clint, and Tara. The four of us—his children—at different stages of our lives.

I was riding on his shoulders at the age of three. Posing with my cousins in our swimsuits at Aunt Eunice's lake house at age eight. Sitting on a couch at age twelve with my dad, Cliff, and Clint. I recognized some of the pictures. I had some of the same prints. The final one of me and the boys was from our last Christmas together, when they were one and two, and were dressed in red footie-pajamas.

There were a few more pictures of just the boys.

And then, pictured by herself in several photos, was Tara. Just a baby.

Most of the book was blank, but on those first few pages we were all in there together, as if we were a real family. As if he'd raised us and knew us and had lived our lives with us. As if he'd cared.

It had hit me in that moment—that moment on that afternoon in October 1996—that he must have cared. Or he wouldn't have made the album.

It struck me the same way now, with the receiver in my hand and Nurse Sally on the line.

Our dad didn't know how to hold on to us in real life, but he'd held on to our pictures because it was all he'd had of us. And because we'd mattered to him.

"Maybe," I said to Nurse Sally, thinking aloud.

"Excuse me?" she asked.

"Maybe others will come," I said, though I had no idea how that would possibly happen.

Time had not stood still where the photo album had stopped.

Cliff was now twenty-five, and I hadn't spoken with him in months. Clint was twenty-four. We hadn't talked in five years. Tara, twenty-one, had grown up within thirty minutes of the boys and our dad, but she'd never expressed an interest in meeting any of them.

The photo album was the only place the four of us had ever been together. But biologically, my dad was theirs as much as he was mine. They needed to know he'd been in an accident.

They needed to know that he could die. And I needed to be the one to tell them.

"Yeah," I said again, mostly to myself, "maybe others will come." A plan began to form.

"Okay then," said Sally, interrupting my thoughts. "I'll make a note of that, and we'll see you Thursday."

CHAPTER 12
A Frenzied Scrawl

APRIL 1984

My sixteen-year-old self was at a loss as to how I could possibly forgive my dad for letting go of Sherry and Tara. How could I carry on as if this hadn't rocked my world?

I don't remember opening any of the presents my dad gave me at Grandma's that Sunday afternoon. Or having a conversation about what had happened. Or staying for long after finding out that my dad and Sherry had separated.

I don't remember saying a word to him as he drove me home. Everything about him had reeked of defeat—his slumped shoulders, his long face, his tired eyes. Had he even tried to keep his new family together? When had he given up hope?

He parked at the curb in front of my house and reached over to hug me goodbye. I let him, but I didn't hug back. I wanted to get out as fast as I could and separate myself from the mess my dad had made of his life.

When I got in the house, I shot straight upstairs to my

room. I yelled a quick hello but didn't seek out my mom and Charlie. They would see the distress on my face and want to know what had happened. I didn't want to be the one to tell them that they'd been right about everything.

I sat in silence on my bed for a long time, weighed down by the pain and sadness of this new loss. I went over questions in my head that no one had given me answers to. What had happened, and why wasn't my dad trying to do anything about it? Why hadn't he told me sooner? Where had Sherry and Tara gone?

Sadness flooded my heart and then turned into anger. Whatever had happened, I was sure my dad was to blame.

I got up, grabbed a notebook and pen from my desk, and turned to a clean page to write.

Dad, I can't do this anymore, I scribbled.

As much as I wanted to believe in him and stick by him, I couldn't accept that he had once again ended important relationships in his life. In my life.

I no longer want to get close to people only to have them ripped out of my life with no notice and through no fault of my own, I wrote.

As much as I wanted to look past his faults, I simply couldn't anymore.

I can't grow up with someone who still needs to grow up himself.

I'd lost my trust in him and needed time to heal without my thoughts being clouded by what he might say to make me believe things could be different. That he could be different.

Don't call me, I wrote. *I don't want to see you anymore. I don't love you anymore.*

I'm sure there was more, and I'm sure it was all written in a frenzied scrawl—unedited, uncensored, raw. I don't know if I signed it, but if I did, I know I didn't write, "*Love, Bessers.*" I never wanted to hear that name again.

I gave the letter to my mom before I left for school on Monday morning. I asked her to read it—partly so she would understand how I felt and partly because I wanted her input. All day at school, I thought about what she'd say, how she might try to dissuade me from sending it, how she might suggest I tone it down. But I was determined to stick to my guns. My dad needed to know how much his failed relationships were hurting me.

I ran upstairs as soon as I got home from school to find my mom putting laundry away in my brother Brett's room. I plunked down on his bed and waited, hoping she was ready to tell me her thoughts.

She slid a stack of Brett's folded t-shirts into one of his drawers.

"Did you read it?" I asked.

She lifted the laundry basket from the floor, rested it on her hip, and turned to look at me.

"Of course I did," she said gently. She turned away before adding, "I put it in the mail this morning." She started toward Brett's doorway.

"What?" I shouted at her, bolting from the bed to follow at her heels. Fear tore through me.

She turned and stared at me, taken aback.

"What do you mean, 'What'?" she asked, ignoring my panicked state. "I mailed it. This morning." She started back toward the door. "Isn't that what you wanted me to do?"

"I didn't mean for you to send it! I just wanted you to read it!" I followed her out the door and down the hallway.

"Well, it was fine." She stopped and turned to face me again. "Really, Gina, it was good. I think he needs to hear what you have to say."

I was stunned. My words—my thoughts and feelings, born of a grieving heart and penned in a pool of tears—were on their way to him. It was done. And oddly, though I was petrified of what his response might be, I was also the tiniest bit relieved. There would be no agonizing over finding the right words, no struggle to decide if I should or shouldn't send it. In many ways, my mom had made it easier. And she thought I was right. That meant everything.

Although I didn't want to hear from my dad because it would make everything so much harder, I waited for his response like I would have waited to hear from a boy I'd broken up with for good reason but still loved deeply. Every time the phone rang, I was sure it would be him, that he was going to try to woo me back with his humor and his charm. I expected him to laugh things off. I even knew the words he would say: "You can't tell me you don't love me. I'm your dad! We love each other. C'mon, Bessers!" And I would desperately want to put up a fight—because I was so hurt and so angry—but I knew that, eventually, I'd give in because everything he said was true.

Of course I loved him. So much it hurt inside. Of course he loved me. I was his little girl. Even at sixteen, I was still his Bessers. All I needed was for him to tell me that everything was going to be okay, and then make it that way. And keep it that way.

Each day I was sure would be the day he'd call. I'd rehearsed what I would say in response to him, just so I could let my thoughts be known before I relented. Each night, I went to bed wondering why he hadn't called yet. As the weeks passed, I wondered if he ever would.

He never did.

His silence stung. It was worse than the loss of Cliff and Clint. It cut deeper than the loss of Sherry and Tara. Though I'd pushed him away, I hadn't wanted him to go. I'd just wanted things to change—for the hurt to stop and for him to understand he was the cause of it.

I still wanted—still needed—the dad who drove with his knees and lit up watching the Eighth Street Bridge open for boats. I still loved the dad who read me my horoscope and sang me his favorite songs. The one who called me Bessers and hugged me like he meant it. It was the dad who drank too much and caused his wives and children to disappear that I wanted to be rid of. The one who canceled Christmas and couldn't be depended on by anyone, not even me.

I would've forgiven him. If only he'd asked. But he didn't, and I had to remind myself that I'd told him not to. Not to call and not to see me. He was complying with my wishes, and I had to cope with the consequences, which this time, meant learning to live without him for more than just a few months.

CHAPTER 13
Eighth Street

AUGUST 1986

More than two years passed without a call from my dad. As far as I knew, he was still living on the other side of town in Sheboygan. I was preparing to move to Florida where my mom and Charlie were relocating with Brett and Rick. I was going, too, so I could live at home while attending college.

Leaving my hometown meant leaving everyone I knew—my friends, aunts, uncles, and cousins. My dad and Grandma. I hadn't seen either of them since the day I'd learned Sherry and Tara were gone, but because I'd be moving a thousand miles away, I couldn't leave without saying a proper goodbye, at least to Grandma. She and I had been in touch through letters during my junior year when I'd been living in Germany as an exchange student, but outside of that, we hadn't corresponded.

My dad had sent a Christmas card my junior year, and I'd opened it hoping to find he'd written an explanation as to why he hadn't called. But all I'd found was his signature. I ripped up the card and envelope and threw them away.

He sent another Christmas card during my senior year and a card for my eighteenth birthday. Maybe I should've been happy he was thinking of me. Maybe I should've felt loved. But each card made me angrier than I already was. At any point, he could've dialed my number or shown up on my doorstep. But over those two years, he'd only shown up in my mailbox in the form of cheap cards that offered no apology.

I hadn't known how to stay connected to Grandma without giving in to my dad, so even though it doubled my pain to not see her, I'd let things be. But I needed to see her before I left. Luckily, she was the one who answered the phone when I called. I would've hung up on him.

We arranged to meet for lunch at our favorite burger joint, The Charcoal Inn, just a few blocks down from her house on Eighth Street. After hugs and kisses and a few tears, we ordered our favorite meal—greasy burgers, complete with Milwaukee Dill Pickles and Heinz Ketchup, and crispy fries. We came away with full tummies and sad faces. Though we'd just reconnected, we knew we wouldn't see each for quite a while. Long-distance phone calls were expensive. Writing letters would have to do.

She and I walked back toward her house, hand-in-hand just like we used to, along the street I knew so well. I thought of the many times we'd stopped at Frederick's Bakery across the street. How many chocolate éclairs I'd eaten while swaying on her front porch swing. I thought of the countless games of Rummy we'd played at her kitchen table and how I loved listening to her tell me about her childhood. I ached thinking of the two years we'd spent apart. I'd missed so much by not coming to visit her. As we walked and I held her frail hand, I ached too for all the years to come, not knowing when I'd see her again, or if I ever would.

"Come in for a little while," she said when we reached the house.

I would've loved nothing more than to sit at her kitchen table, play cards, and top off my burger with a fudge-royal-ice-cream sundae, but I was stopped by the sight of a dilapidated van parked out in front. It was right behind my car. It hadn't been there when we'd left.

It had to be his.

Had he been living with her all this time, or had he timed this visit just right?

Had she set me up?

I stopped walking and turned to look at her. She looked down, confirming my suspicion that my dad was in the house, and then she gently squeezed my hand, perhaps to give me assurance that everything would be okay if I went in. That she'd stay by my side.

I felt three feet tall.

I didn't want to let go of her hand.

I didn't want to see him.

"Please?" Grandma said softly. "He just wants to say goodbye."

I followed her up the porch steps, through the front screen door, and down the narrow hallway, which still reeked of cigarette smoke, to her living room. My eyes went first to the sugar-coated orange slices in their crystal dish, right where they always were on the living room table. I didn't stop to pop one in my mouth.

My dad was standing in the doorway between the living room and the kitchen, his six-foot frame taking up most of the space. Beyond him, I could see the kitchen table where we'd sat to celebrate my sixteenth birthday, the last time I'd been in the house. He tilted his head, and his dark blond bangs fell across his forehead. He looked at me. He seemed different. Older. Disheveled. Sad.

"Hi, Bessers," he said, but his voice didn't have the same lilt that I remembered. It lacked happiness. And hope. He took a couple slow steps in my direction as though he were wading through rough waters and it would be difficult for him to reach me.

"Hi," I said back, guarded, not wanting to make it any easier.

"I hear you're moving," he said.

I nodded, not knowing what to say. As far as I was concerned, there was nothing for me to say. He was the one who needed to do the talking.

I wanted him to apologize for not calling. Explain why he'd let me slip out of his life. I wanted to hear him say he understood how his irresponsible behavior and drinking had driven away people I loved and that he was sorry he'd let that happen. That he understood how much that had hurt me.

I wanted him to say he'd do better, if not for himself, then for me—because he was my dad, and I was his Bessers, and even though he'd screwed up in the past, he would be there for me from now on, no matter what.

"I just wanted to say goodbye," he said.

Our eyes met. I realized I still meant something to him, but it wasn't enough.

I nodded again. He'd given me up. Just like he'd given up my siblings. I'd thought I was special. We had sixteen years of history, but he'd let me go just the same. My disappointment in him overshadowed the love that still lingered within me.

My head started to throb.

"I've gotta go." I turned toward the front hallway.

"I came to your graduation," he said.

That stopped me for a moment. I'd had no idea. I didn't want to care.

"I saw you, but you didn't see me."

I turned back and looked at his rugged face, into the blue eyes I remembered.

"I took Grandma," he said. "I was real proud of you that day."

That set me off.

You don't get to be proud of me, were the words that shot into my head. *I am what I am in spite of you.*

So angry. So hurt. *If you care so much, why didn't you fight for me?*

"I'm gonna go." I turned to leave. He stepped closer and leaned in to hug me. I leaned in and let him, accepting the gesture for what I saw it as—an ending. Not a new beginning.

I didn't know if I'd ever see him again.

Grandma walked me out to the front porch, and we stopped to wrap our arms around each other in a hug. Was this the last time I'd see either of them? After spending all my life in the Midwest, Florida seemed as far away as a distant planet.

I peeked at the front porch swing over her shoulder, then pulled out of our embrace and kissed her on the cheek.

Don't cry, I thought. *This isn't goodbye forever. You'll write to her. You'll come back and see her.*

I made my way down the steps to the sidewalk of Eighth Street and turned back to see Grandma watching me. My dad had stayed inside.

I would write to her many times from Florida, and she would write back. I wouldn't hear from him at all—not a card, letter, or call—and I was determined to be fine with that.

CHAPTER 14
My Little Game

APRIL 1989

I thought living a thousand miles away from my dad would bring me peace, that the distance would make it easier to live separate lives. Since he wasn't right across town, there was no pressure to reconnect, and we had an excellent excuse for not seeing each other. I didn't want to reach out, but the silence nagged at me.

Grandma had written during my first two years of college, updating me on my aunts, uncles, and cousins, and on her deteriorating health, but she never mentioned him. I assumed she was just being careful. Straddling the line.

As my twenty-first birthday approached, a thought came into my head—if I heard from him, if he sent me a card for *this* birthday, I'd make contact. It was a silly—and safe—thing to tell myself because as far as I knew, neither he nor Grandma had my current address. The summer before my junior year, I'd moved six hours north of my mom and Charlie to attend Florida State University in Tallahassee, and I hadn't written to her since.

If my dad sent a card for this birthday, I wouldn't rip it up. I'd take it as a sign, and I'd call to break the silence.

I thought back to the birthday gifts he'd given me when I was a child. A stuffed animal—a big gray raccoon—and a transistor radio when I turned nine. An acoustic guitar when I was ten and a charm bracelet when I turned eleven. I had loved them all. He'd known me so well. He'd been such a loving and thoughtful father. What had happened to make him such an absent one?

I needed to know.

I didn't expect him to win my little game, of course. He didn't even know he was playing. And if he didn't meet my challenge, it would just strengthen my argument against him. Reaffirm that he didn't care about me, and I'd have every right to continue being angry with him. But sure enough, on the day of my twenty-first birthday, the card came in the mail.

My name and my Tallahassee address were written on the envelope in his distinctive script. The return address was Grandma's house on Eighth Street. I opened it.

On the front of the card was a picture of a young woman walking through a field of flowers.

For Your Twenty-First Birthday, it said.

I flipped the card to look inside. He'd signed it, "DAD," in all caps and with quotation marks, which to my English-major mind was interpreted as *I'm your dad*, hence the caps. *But only if you're willing*, hence the quotation marks. He probably hadn't thought that through, but it made me smile.

This time, I took his signature as assurance that he meant the words in the card, even if he hadn't written them:

With a wish for every happiness. A bright beginning of a year when every day will bring

new friends, achievements and new happiness your way. For the future waits for you,

shining with the promise of your wishes coming true.

Below "DAD," he'd written, *Have a nice day.*

The card contained no apology or explanation, but as I'd promised myself, I did not tear it up. I was ready to do things differently. Maybe he'd sent the card because he was ready to do things differently too.

From the return address, I assumed he was still living with Grandma on Eighth Street, and I still knew her number by heart. I dialed it immediately, and he answered on the first ring.

"Hello?"

His voice brought me back to my childhood. I pictured him sitting on the arm of Grandma's couch in the living room where the sugared orange slices sat in the candy dish on the table. I imagined him holding the receiver of her old-fashioned, rotary-dial telephone to his ear.

"Hi." I waited for his reaction. Would he recognize my voice?

"Hi, Bessers," he said softly.

I smiled—because he knew it was me and because this time I was happy to hear him call me by that name again.

"I got your card."

"Oh, good," he said. "Happy Birthday."

I thanked him, and we made small talk. He was still working odd jobs, still installing flooring. He was living with Grandma and taking care of her. He put her on the phone, and she wished me a happy birthday, too. She couldn't get around like she used to, she said. Couldn't just hop on the bus to go shopping at Prange's or Piggly Wiggly. She didn't even cross the street to go to Frederick's Bakery anymore.

"Do you remember those chocolate éclairs?" she asked. Of course I did, I told her.

She wished me happy birthday again, and I wondered if she'd forgotten she already had. Her memory was fading, my dad told me when he got back on the line. She wasn't doing so well. We ran out of things to catch up on and were left with the option of ending the conversation or talking about everything. I chose everything.

"Remember that letter I wrote you when I was sixteen?" I began.

"Of course," he said.

"Why did you never respond?" There, I'd said it—the question that had been burning in my mind for the last five years.

"I did respond," he said.

"What?" That made no sense. "What are you talking about? You never called."

"I did call."

My mind spun. Had I missed the call? Was he lying?

"Your mother answered," he said. "And then she came to see me."

He couldn't see my jaw drop. How could that be true?

"My mom came to see you?" I asked, trying to imagine my mom walking up the front porch steps of Grandma's house and down the narrow hallway that led to the living room where my dad sat now. Trying to imagine my mom and dad talking.

"What did she say?"

"She told me you were very upset."

"I was."

"I know," he said gently. "I read your letter. My life was a mess, Bessers."

He wasn't exactly apologizing, but I took it as his way of saying he'd screwed up. It meant so much that he'd finally admitted it.

"I know," I said. "I was there."

We both let out a nervous laugh.

"Why didn't you call me after you talked with her?" I asked.

"I thought it would be better not to. You had a good life. You didn't need me messing it up."

I sighed at this bittersweet revelation. He'd left my life in order to lessen my pain, but his absence had only increased it.

"Your mom said I needed to step up or step out."

"So you stepped out."

Had my mom expected him to step up instead? I was glad she'd come to my defense but floored that she'd never told me.

"I never stopped thinking about you," he said.

I closed my eyes and took that in. What would've happened if I'd answered his call instead of my mom? I'd never know. But at least now I knew he'd called. He'd cared. He'd cared all along.

Our conversation moved on to the English and education classes I was taking to become a high-school teacher and how living in Florida was different from living in Wisconsin.

"I'm so proud of you," he said.

This time, I let him be. I knew he meant it, and I was glad he was.

"I was surprised to get your card," I told him before we hung up. I didn't mention that he'd won the crazy game I'd cooked up in my head.

"I never forget your birthday," he said. "I think back to the day you were born every year."

It was nice to know I'd never been far from his thoughts.

After our call, I sat in silence for a long while, feeling at peace with our relationship. We'd started a new chapter, and I expected we'd stay in touch. He'd sounded like the dad I remembered, the one who loved me—and for a few minutes I'd been his little girl again and I liked the way that felt.

Over the next year, we exchanged a few letters and phone calls. Christmas and birthday cards were sent. But he fell silent as I neared my spring graduation from Florida State. Grandma died the following month.

I didn't know about her death until a couple days after the funeral when my dad called to tell me she'd passed.

I wouldn't know until many years later that her house on Eighth Street went into foreclosure, which made my dad homeless.

All I knew was that the calls and letters stopped.

We'd lost touch.

And I tried to fill the void left by his absence in all the wrong ways.

CHAPTER 15
The Tarnished Mirror

MAY 1990

By the time I was twenty-two, my relationship with my dad wasn't the only one not working out for me. And he wasn't the only one of us who had a drinking problem.

I'd met Mark at the beginning of my junior year in college, and by the time I graduated two years later, we'd broken up and gotten back together enough times that I should've known moving in with him was a bad idea. He had a biting sense of humor, often at my expense, and I'd spent much of our time together vacillating between feeling insecure about myself and believing him when he said no one would ever love me like he did.

Though I'd interviewed for multiple teaching positions, not one was offered to me. Wanting to stay in Tallahassee with Mark limited my options. Instead, I tucked away my English Education degree and got my college job back, working at the local newspaper. Mark worked there, too—second shift. I worked days, which made it easy to go out and party without him. And as our relationship deteriorated and my self-esteem plummeted, it made it easy to find affection elsewhere. I lost track of the number of times.

I moved out within two months of moving in, and after a few months of trial and error, started dating a guy I really liked —who then cheated on me. I wanted to stay in the relationship anyway, hoping he'd see I was the better choice. He declined my offer.

Work, party, sleep, repeat. That was my routine, with more random guys thrown in to help me pass the time. None of them held my interest for long. Until Aaron.

I met him in Tallahassee a year after graduation. Though I'd already lined up a high-school teaching position in Daytona Beach, Aaron and I enjoyed a few good months together. He was leaving Tallahassee, too, to work for the summer in Alaska. I'd be away teaching by the time he returned.

We were both at odd places in our lives. I was out of touch with my dad, and Aaron's father had just passed away in his early fifties from cancer. We didn't talk about either father. I was in limbo, waiting for my teaching career to begin and planning to head off to a new city. He was finishing college, not ready to settle down. He made it clear that we would part ways and not do that long-distance thing.

He left for Alaska a month before my move to Daytona. He called and wrote. I hadn't expected that. We touched base every few days. He brought up the idea of me visiting him for a week and paid half the price of the ticket.

The night I arrived, after we'd reacquainted ourselves, I'd professed my love for him. He said he didn't feel the same. I felt dirty. And used. Sure that he'd asked me to visit only so he could sleep with me. As if what we'd shared and who I was as a person didn't matter at all.

On the heels of that trip, I moved to The Spring Break Capital of the World.

I was twenty-three and had been hired to instruct six theater classes, direct the school plays, and lead the drama club. It was my dream job, and my head was filled with idealistic visions of what my future would hold. But as a Wisconsin girl who'd worked through every spring break in high school and college, and who was looking for love, the opportunity to spend each weekend meeting new people and partying on the beach was too hard to resist.

I became best friends with my school's music teacher, Laura, a girl my age who was also new to Daytona and had grown up in Wisconsin. We were a natural pair—young, single, busty, and blonde—and we frequented our favorite beach bar, The Ocean Deck, which was just fifteen minutes away from my apartment.

Time spent perfecting lesson plans and grading papers quickly gave way to days spent on the sand and evenings filled with live reggae, bottomless pitchers of beer, and cheap tequila shots. The endless supply of college boys and having bartenders who knew us by name added to the attraction. I was looking for love, but most of them were just looking for a good time. Most of the time, I was too drunk to care.

By the time our school's spring break rolled around the first week of April, Laura and I were entrenched in beach life. In honor of our beloved bar, we got air-brushed shirts that proclaimed we were "Deck-a-holics." We rented a motel room on the beach, so we wouldn't have to drive home all week. I contemplated ditching my teaching gig to become a server.

In May, Laura bought a little place just a mile from the bar. Our very own beach shack! It sat empty while she was repainting the interior and preparing to move, but on a weekend near the end of the school year, we decided to stay the night sans furniture. We brought sleeping bags and were excited to christen the place.

That Saturday had started like every other. The

temperature was in the high eighties, and we spent the entire afternoon alternately tanning on the beach and cooling off in the bar, where we danced and drank tequila. A few of our friends joined us when the sun went down. By the end of the night, however, I'd lost track of them all.

Near closing time, I stepped into the ladies' room to pee and run my finger under the tight elastic of my tiger-striped bikini top. I'd thrown a crop top and skirt on over my suit earlier in the night, so I didn't have to go back to Laura's to get changed. Coming out of the stall, I caught a glimpse of my reflection in the tarnished mirror above the sink and stood there admiring myself.

Nice tan.

I splashed my face with cold water from the tap, pulled my sun-streaked hair into a disheveled ponytail, and stumbled back into the bar. Through the dim light, I searched for the faces of my friends.

Seeing no one familiar, I approached a foursome huddled around a table. A girl in the group nudged her friend and pointed at my shoe. They laughed and walked away. I threw a dirty look in their direction, noticed the toilet paper trailing from my shoe, and bent down to pick it up. Teetering on my way back up, I grabbed the closest bar stool and took a seat. I scanned the room again.

Laura was my ride home. I was staying at her house.

I searched the remaining faces in a panic. It was only one-thirty. *What the hell?*

Had she left me?

I was pissed.

How could she do that?

What did she expect me to do?

It didn't enter my mind that maybe she'd looked for me but couldn't find me. Or that maybe she was just tired of taking care of me. More than once on our weekends out, I'd abandoned her when something (or someone) better had come along. More than once, I'd ended the night on a cold bathroom floor, pressing my face against the tiles, and she'd been the one to hold my hair back over the toilet.

None of that came to me.

I popped off the bar stool and stormed out of the bar into the night.

How dare she!

I'd walk the mile to her house, get in my car, and drive home. I didn't need her.

I headed down the sidewalk on State Road A1A, Daytona's main drag, and passed the Taco Bell we frequented at the end of most nights. A quick glance in that direction told me she wasn't there.

A few blocks down, I turned onto a dark side road. Feeling vulnerable and concerned that someone might take advantage of the situation, I picked up the pace. I made it to Laura's unscathed and decided to confront her before driving off. So what if it was two in the morning. She'd left me. So what if she was asleep. She deserved to be woken up.

I marched up the steps and banged on the front door.

No answer.

I banged again and yelled her name.

Nothing.

Either she'd gone to sleep without worrying about my well-being or she'd heard me and was ignoring me.

Oh, fuck her.

I headed to my car, digging deep in my pockets for my keys. A scrunched-up dollar bill and my license was all I came up with. I twirled around to scan the ground for my keys but got dizzy.

"Damn it!" I said aloud, realizing I'd probably left them at the bar.

If I hurried, I figured I could make it back before the staff finished cleaning and locked up but going back to the bar meant I'd have to walk past the stragglers on the street again. Two more times—there and back.

Maybe someone at the bar will give me a ride back here, I thought, *or let me crash at their place.*

Three employees were still working when I got there, and I counted myself lucky to know them all.

"Hey!" I said, walking in like I owned the place.

A bartender who'd cheated on his girlfriend with me was totaling money at the register. He glanced up at me and then quickly looked back down to continue counting. A server I'd gone home with a couple times was stacking chairs on tables. He and his new girlfriend, another server at the bar, looked my way but pretended they hadn't heard me. They went back to focusing on their jobs.

"Are my keys here?" I asked numbly to no one in particular. No one answered back.

I scowled at them, feeling betrayed one minute and ashamed the next.

I'd loved that bar. It had become my second home. I'd thought the people there were my friends. It was clear now, even in my drunken state, that they weren't. They never had been.

Hours before, I'd so foolishly primped in front of the bathroom's tarnished mirror, admiring my reflection, feeling pretty. What I saw now was a true reflection of myself, and it was anything but.

I turned without another word and started back to Laura's, no longer caring about the stragglers on the street. I wasn't afraid of them. I had become one of them. And that's what scared me the most.

Back at her place, I knocked again at the door. My earlier anger gave way to panic—without my keys, I couldn't drive home. I needed a place to stay. No one answered.

The impact of the sun, the booze, the walking, and the worry had taken its toll on me.

Maybe Laura went back to her apartment, I reasoned. Maybe she didn't want to spend the night on the floor.

But it looked like I was going to. Exhaustion had set in, and I slunk down on the sandy porch, grabbed a dirty beach towel from the floor to cover myself, and laid my head to rest on Laura's front doormat.

A stray cat nestled near me at some point during the night, and I woke to its soft purring and its loose fur sticking to my lips. I peeled my sunburned face from the prickly bristles of the mat and rubbed sand off my sweaty arms. I listened for movement in the house but heard nothing. I was alone.

Rolling over to shield my eyes from the light of a new day, I noticed the sun reflecting off a shiny object a few feet from me on the porch. I sat up to get a better look.

My car keys.

They'd been on the porch all along.

It was time to leave Daytona.

Part Three

CHAPTER 16
I Have a Dad

DECEMBER 10, 2003

My dad is dying. It was my waking thought Wednesday morning—the day after the accident, the day before I would see him at Froedtert Hospital. I nestled under my comforter, procrastinating the preparation I needed to do that day—packing, writing notes for my mother-in-law who'd be watching our children, and making calls to my siblings to find out if they might want to meet me in Milwaukee.

My dad is dying. The thought wouldn't leave my head. I rolled onto my back and stared up at the bedroom ceiling. *Was he dying though? Was he really?* I'd committed myself to going to the hospital, but part of me still hoped he'd wake up before I left home or at least before I got to his bedside.

It was nearly nine o'clock before I started on my tasks for the day. My dad had been at the hospital for about twelve hours. I called the hospital to check on his condition, hoping there'd been a change for the better—a small sign, a slight movement, *anything*—to make the situation a little less urgent.

"He's still unresponsive," the nurse on duty said. She shared that the CT scan they'd run the night before had shown a significant collection of blood on the surface of his brain, and there was a contusion within the right frontal lobe.

"But his tubes are in place and fluid is draining," she assured me.

I pictured my dad lying in his bed with red and black tubes —like thin strands of licorice rope—running from his head and chest to the machines that monitored his every move. They stabilized his heartbeat, his breathing, his comfort level. For all I knew, they were the only things keeping him alive.

I hung up with the nurse but kept the phone in my hand for the next call I needed to make. It was time to put my plan into action. I'd try Tara first. Of my three half-siblings, she'd be the easiest to reach. Whether she'd be interested in going, I didn't know.

I dialed her number, wondering if she'd pick up or if I'd get Sherry. Tara was twenty-one, living at home, and working full-time at a tanning salon. I'd been in touch with Sherry since my junior year in high school when I'd written to her from Germany and she'd written back. It had been the first time we'd been in touch since her separation from my dad. They'd been divorced for nearly a year, and Tara was almost three.

In my letter to Sherry, I must've shared what had transpired after their separation and asked to reconnect with her and Tara. After not having seen them for more than two years—and fearing that Sherry might cut me out of their lives as Debra had—Sherry's response was like a warm hug.

I'm so sorry to hear how brokenhearted Roy has left you, she'd written. *I wish I could've done more to make things easier for you. I don't ever want you to think you're interrupting our lives. I've always loved you as a stepdaughter, if not my real daughter. Don't ever think we don't love you.*

She sent a few pictures of Tara—one from the previous

Christmas, one of her in a kiddie pool that summer, and one of her dressed up in a lilac outfit, wearing a fancy white Easter hat and carrying a little purse. She was blonde and blue-eyed, just like I'd been at that age. My dad's features shone in her face. I kissed each picture of my little sister and pinned them to my bedroom wall so I could see her every day.

Sherry said we'd set up a time to get together when I got back to Sheboygan, and we did. I visited Sherry and Tara multiple times during my senior year, and after I moved to Florida, Sherry sent letters and pictures until Tara was old enough to write and send them herself.

The three of us had seen each other a number of times over the years when I'd traveled back to Sheboygan to visit friends and other family members. When Tara was fourteen, she and Sherry had traveled to Florida, along with Sherry's sister and their father, to attend my wedding to Larry. Tara had been one of our bridesmaids.

I'd last seen her two years earlier when she was eighteen and had just graduated from high school. Larry and I had flown her down to stay with us for a week at the beach.

The Wednesday morning I called to let her know about our dad's accident, she wasn't home. Sherry answered.

Tara was at work, she said, and she already knew about the accident. A woman from Sheboygan Memorial had called their house the night before as well. Sherry was still listed as an emergency contact for my dad though they'd been divorced for nearly twenty years.

She was surprised to hear I was going to Milwaukee and said she'd have Tara call me when she got home.

Would Tara want to go? Maybe to see me, but maybe not if it meant seeing him. I thought back to her visit to Florida and what she'd said when I'd broached the subject.

On one of the first days of our beach trip, the two of us had taken a kayak out into the Gulf of Mexico to look for dolphins and catch up on our lives. Our talk eventually turned to our dads. We had five of them between us—my two and her three.

On a trip back to Wisconsin in 1993, I'd met Brian, Sherry's second husband. He'd adopted Tara when she was in elementary school. She'd been living in the same neighborhood I'd lived in from fourth through twelfth grade, her backyard butting up against my old backyard, and she was attending the same school I'd attended.

A few years later, on another trip back to Wisconsin when Tara was in middle school, I met Tim—Sherry's third husband. He was Tara's stepdad but treated her like a daughter.

Even though Tara didn't remember our dad—she'd been only a couple of years old when he'd stopped visiting her—and though she'd never expressed an interest in meeting him, I thought that maybe now that she was eighteen, verging on adulthood, she might be ready, curious, looking for closure. I didn't know where he was because he and I hadn't been in touch for nearly five years, but they lived in the same city—maybe she could track him down.

"Would you like to meet him?" I asked, pulling my oar up to float on the waves.

"I *have* a dad," she'd said with no hesitation.

She'd dismissed the idea so quickly, I wondered what was lying under the surface. Was she really content with never meeting him? Or was she angry—like I'd been for so long—thinking he didn't care enough to reach out, so why should she?

I didn't know which dad Tara had been referring to when she'd said she *had* a dad, but I knew which one she looked like, and it wasn't either of them. I felt sad for both Tara and my dad. At least I'd been in his life for sixteen years. At least I'd known him. She was his daughter as much as I was and yet they were complete strangers. Worse yet, they might never meet.

I let the subject go and asked about college and what she'd been up to recently. She'd start classes in the fall, she said, and she got a job at a tanning salon. She rattled off her likes and dislikes, and then she threw a curveball into our conversation.

"I love Elvis!"

She was facing forward at the front of the kayak, so she couldn't see the smile that broke out on my face.

I loved Elvis, too.

So did our dad.

He'd learned to play Elvis's songs on his guitar, and he sang them for me into his microphone with his amps on high. Elvis had been his idol.

I'd been nine when Elvis died. But Tara hadn't even been born yet. And she *loved* him? Maybe it was genetic.

She and I paddled along under the summer sun, and my mind drifted back to the best gift my dad had ever given me. On a cold autumn night when I was in the eighth grade, he'd taken me to the Sheboygan County Fair and tried his luck at a toss-the-ring-on-the-bottle game. People typically lose this tricky gamble, but that night—after multiple tries—my dad won. And he got to choose a prize.

"That mirror!" He pointed to a one-foot-square mirror that had Elvis's young face emblazoned on it. "That's what I want!" It must've caught his eye as we walked by. It was likely the reason he'd stopped to play the game.

After he celebrated his victory with a beer or two, we headed back to Grandma's house. After we climbed the porch steps, he took a left and plunked down on the aluminum couch swing. He patted the seat next to him for me to join him, and I obliged even though the wind was picking up and we'd already been outside in the cold for hours.

He held up the mirror, slanting it this way and that—so the

light from the streetlamps would hit it just right. He looked at me intently, cocked his head, and asked with a slur in his speech, "Did you know Elvis sold more than three hundred million albums?"

I hadn't known, but he hadn't been waiting for my answer anyway.

"Three hundred and twelve million!" he exclaimed. "Man, he was the *greatest*. He was the *King*."

For a moment he seemed lost in thought. Then suddenly, he thrust the mirror in my direction.

"Here—I want you to have this."

I was shocked. I mean, this was *Elvis*. He'd worked hard to win it. And he was giving it to *me*. I wasn't cold anymore.

"Write that down," he said, pointing at Elvis's picture.

"Write what down?" I asked, holding the mirror in my hands for the first time. I ran my fingers over the smooth surface, over Elvis's pretty face.

"Three hundred and twelve million albums sold."

What was he thinking? We were on the front porch in the middle of the night, and there was nothing to write with.

"On the back," he said, unaware of my confusion.

"I don't have a pen."

He looked dumbfounded.

"Ah, well then." He shrugged his shoulders and started to rock the swing. "Write it down when you get home, okay? And never forget it. He was the King of Rock 'n Roll."

I wrote it on the back of the mirror the very next day when I got home.

And I never forgot it.

I didn't share that story with Tara. She didn't know our dad loved Elvis. I could've told her, but I thought she might think I was trying too hard to make a connection.

"I love Elvis, too," was all I'd said.

Two years later—the day before I'd fly to Milwaukee—I

didn't know any more about Tara's state of mind regarding our dad than I'd known that day at the beach. In our letters and phone calls, she hadn't mentioned him once. And I hadn't asked.

Maybe she would come to the hospital to see me. Maybe she would be willing to see him. But maybe she wouldn't see the need.

I *have* a dad, she'd said.

All I could do was wait for her call.

CHAPTER 17
Three T's

FALL 1993

I made no effort to see my dad when I visited Sheboygan in the fall of 1993. I hadn't heard from him for more than two years. He didn't know I'd lived in Daytona or that I'd taught for a year. He didn't know I'd moved back to Tallahassee when the school year ended or that I'd met Larry, and we'd fallen in love, shortly after my return.

Looking back, I realize Grandma's death must've sent my dad into a tailspin. He'd lost the home he'd lived in most of his life, and with that, he'd likely lost any sense of stability. Most importantly, he'd lost his mom, who had been his biggest supporter.

By the time I was twenty-five, I'd come to a certain kind of acceptance regarding my relationship with my dad. I'd convinced myself that I didn't need or want him in my life. I made myself believe that I was better off without him. The thought of reconnecting with him, which would have meant searching for him while I was in Wisconsin, had seemed a waste of my time and emotional energy. And what would I have said if I'd found him? I couldn't make him stay in touch with me.

I didn't want to worry about any of that. Larry was coming with me, visiting my hometown for the first time. I was excited to show him my childhood home and my old schools, and of course, I wanted to introduce him to other family and friends who lived in Sheboygan and Manitowoc.

Cliff and Clint came to mind. It was time to find them.

It had been twelve years since I'd called their grandmother, Rose, and had asked to give them Christmas gifts. I had never made another attempt to connect. They were fourteen and fifteen years old now—still a few years away from the mandatory eighteen, but with my trip to Sheboygan planned and Larry by my side, I felt emboldened to act. I wanted to know where they lived, but what I wanted most was to see them.

The first time I'd called Rose, back when I was thirteen, I'd been so sure she would help me. This time, I was less confident but determined not to take no for an answer.

Once again, I dove into the pages of my little pink address book, found her number, and dialed.

She answered on the third ring, her voice just as soft and sweet as I remembered.

I told her I'd be coming to Sheboygan in a few months and that I wanted to see the boys.

She didn't reply right away, and her hesitancy made me nervous.

Not again. Not after all this time.

But I was ready if she said no. Prepared to press her a bit, plead my case.

"They go to a place called Three T's. They like to hang out there."

I held my breath, letting her words hang in the air. I didn't speak—or move—for fear of messing up this moment or making her change her mind.

"I can tell them to be there on a certain day, at a certain time."

Oh, my God. I was so relieved. Finally, I'd get to reunite with my brothers.

"They know about you and your dad," she said.

I'd thought it odd of her to say that. Why wouldn't they?

"They'll be very interested to meet you." She paused. "But Debra can't know."

All these years later, it was still a thing. Eighteen was eighteen. She'd meant it.

The sky was overcast when Larry and I arrived in Manitowoc on an October afternoon. It looked as if someone had set the dimmer switch too low. The interior of Three T's was even dimmer.

Larry and I entered the place—a restaurant/bar with bowling lanes and pool tables—and gave our eyes a moment to adjust to the darkness. Then my eyes went straight to two teenage boys shooting pool. My world went quiet.

One boy was taller than the other, but they resembled each other, and I could see my dad's face in each of theirs. They were dressed in color-coordinated, oversized clothes that looked brand new. One wore a blue and red varsity jacket with white shorts. The other wore a blue and red Chicago Bears sweatshirt with white jeans. They were a matched set, and I couldn't take my eyes off them.

There were introductions and hugs, but I don't remember our first words. I only remember the feeling of completeness. My heart was whole again.

The four of us played pool and talked for hours that afternoon, quickly getting over the awkwardness of being strangers and leaning into the knowledge that we were family.

I learned the boys had lived near me the whole time I'd lived in Sheboygan. After the divorce from our dad, Debra had moved just a few miles from Grandma's house on Eighth Street. A few years later, they'd moved to Manitowoc, within a mile of my Gramma Joe's house. They'd been right under my nose all along.

"We didn't know about you until about five years ago," Cliff told us.

"Yeah," said Clint. "We thought Mike was our dad." Mike was Debra's second husband, the man who'd adopted them.

I was shocked to hear this.

"How'd you find out?" I asked.

"Grandma," said Cliff, referring to Rose. "When we were in like fourth and fifth grade, we went to Burger King one day with her and Grandpa, and I overheard them talking. Clint and I were sitting at one table, and they were at a table behind us. We knew Mom and Mike were getting divorced, and I heard Grandma say to Grandpa, 'I knew this marriage wasn't gonna last—just like the last one.'"

Larry and I looked at each other. I shook my head.

"I asked Grandma about it later and tried to get her to tell me more," Cliff said, "but she said I should talk to Mom. So I did."

We took a break from playing pool to get some sodas and a snack.

"After I talked to Mom," Cliff continued over french fries, "Grandma told us about Roy and you, and how you'd called years before and had wanted to send us Christmas presents. But she told us we were strictly forbidden from seeing you. That we had to wait until we were eighteen." He shrugged. "That's the way things were."

Until now. I smiled at the sight of them in front of me. *Thank you, Rose.*

"We talked to Roy, too," Clint told us.

"What!" *How was that possible?* "When? How?"

"When Grandma Wilsing died," Cliff said.

I was surprised they even knew about that. They'd been around ten and eleven at that time.

"Our grandma still talked with her sometimes, and when she found out she'd passed away, she called the house and let us talk to Roy."

Rose had broken the silence to let the boys console him. I could only imagine his surprise at hearing their voices. Grandma Wilsing had never mentioned to me that she'd kept up a relationship with Rose. Maybe Grandma had known how —and where—the boys were all along.

"Then Roy called back one day and asked to talk to us again," Clint said.

"Yeah," added Cliff. "Mom found out, and that was the end of that."

I bet.

My dad hadn't told me about this call. Maybe it had happened after he'd called me following Grandma's death. I found it comforting to know that he, too, had reconnected with the boys before they were eighteen.

I looked across the table at my two brothers and smiled. My dad and I had each found a way around Debra, and that felt mighty satisfying.

We ended our afternoon together with hugs and a promise to keep in touch. Even though I'd be heading back to Florida, and we'd have to keep our relationship a secret, I had Cliff and Clint back. It was a new beginning.

CHAPTER 18
Please Hold

WINTER 1993

A couple of months after my trip to Wisconsin in the fall of 1993, I found myself staring into my father's eyes—not in person, but in my baby book. I was flipping through the pages looking for answers as to what life was like during my youngest years. It was an exercise the therapist I was seeing had suggested.

I had gone to counseling that winter not because of my dad —we were through—but because of the high anxiety I felt around my stepdad, Charlie. I'd always felt it. As far back as I could remember.

Charlie liked to remind me about one of our first encounters when I was four. I didn't remember it, of course, but it had stuck with him. He told it the same way every time.

"I wanted to take you for an ice cream cone," he'd say.

He wasn't a natural with kids—even at my young age, I'd probably figured that out. He was a serious businessman, always dressed for work in a three-piece suit and tie. He was out of his element with me but trying to be nice, I imagine, because he was in love with my mother, and we were a package deal.

He would chuckle as he told the story because he knew the ending, and no matter how many times he told it, he couldn't believe the outcome.

"You wouldn't go!" he'd say, throwing up his hands in the air, flabbergasted all over again. "What kid doesn't want to go for an ice cream cone?"

I'd rejected his offer, and I don't think he ever got over that.

What I got from his story was that I was to blame for our relationship not working out. He'd tried. Perhaps if I'd gone with him for an ice cream cone, we would've clicked.

As a child, I'd felt so intimidated by him. As an adult—I was twenty-five when I went to counseling for the first time—I wanted to know how to turn off the switch. How to not take everything he said so personally. How to establish boundaries and not let my choices be governed by his judgment of them.

My therapist and I talked about those things, and then she handed me a book, the one with the exercises in it that had led me to look through my baby book. That had led me to my dad's face.

I came across the flash of his smile beaming from a family portrait taken at our church when I was a baby. He wore a dark suit and thin 1960's-style tie and looked terribly handsome posing with me and my mom. He was twenty-four, she was twenty-two, and their family life was just beginning. In a photo from my first Christmas, he was holding my little hands, helping me to balance on wobbly legs. At two years old, I was riding on his shoulders. The last picture of the three of us was taken on my third birthday. On the day of my fourth, my mom left for the last time. There are no pictures of that birthday in my baby book. By the time I turned five, my mom had met Charlie, and the rest of the family pictures included him.

My relationship with both of my "dads" had been challenging—but there were even more reasons than that for wanting counseling.

By the time I was twenty-five, I'd moved a total of twenty times, including the ten times I'd moved as a child. As an adult, I'd had fourteen different roommates, and after the disastrous relationships I'd had prior to and during my time in Daytona, I knew it was time to settle down and figure some shit out.

Near the end of my time in Daytona, I'd been so depressed, I'd called a suicide hotline—not because I was going to do myself harm, but because I knew I needed help. The woman who answered asked if I'd please hold. That made me laugh. Finding humor in something, even in my depressed state, let me know that I was going to be okay. But being okay and knowing how to move forward were two different things.

I knew I was capable of having healthy relationships. I was close with my mom, and I'd had boyfriends in high school who'd been kind and loving. But my twenties had been such a train wreck, I worried that old patterns would creep up in my relationship with Larry, and I'd sabotage it. I didn't want to. I'd known Larry was the one for me from the start.

Early in our relationship, we'd taken a road trip to Atlanta. We were singing along to our favorite songs while he drove and I navigated. With no GPS, he was relying on me for directions, and we missed a turn.

My mind flashed to being a child in the backseat of our family car. My mom always navigated while Charlie drove. A missed exit would throw Charlie into a tizzy. There'd be swearing and admonishment, jabs at her level of incompetence.

Wincing, I let Larry know we'd missed our turn. Silently berating myself, I waited for the fallout.

"Oh, well," Larry said. "We'll turn around at the next exit." He went back to singing. No raising his voice. No disparaging comments.

The relief I felt was overwhelming. He'd shown me there was another way to handle life's little mishaps.

I'd always thought there must be.

At this same time in my life, Larry's mother told us about a weekend course called, "Understanding Yourself and Others." It was offered every month at a place in town called the Global Relationship Center. Larry and I were doing fine as a couple, but as individuals in our twenties, we were still working through some things. We'd go on different weekends, allowing each of us to have a private experience, but we'd learn the same techniques for communicating and letting go of beliefs and patterns that were no longer serving us.

I attended the course shortly before my twenty-sixth birthday. After going to weekly counseling sessions for several months prior to it, I was primed and ready to get the final answers I needed to have a better relationship with Charlie—but just like the exercises in my self-help book, the exercises in the weekend course led me right back to my dad.

CHAPTER 19
What's Behind Your I?

APRIL 1994

The "Understanding Yourself and Others" course was different from any counseling therapy I'd ever experienced. It took place in a large resource center—a sparse room filled with people I didn't know. I was one of twelve students. There were two instructors—one man and one woman—and around thirty volunteers. They were all former students who'd come to assist us. The course ran from six o'clock Friday night until eight o'clock Sunday evening, minus the time we returned home to sleep each night.

Friday night began with team-building exercises. For one of them, the eleven other students and I worked in unison to lift a seated man four feet off the ground—using only our fingertips! It was astonishing to see what we could accomplish through excellent communication and by focusing on working as a team. These skills, we were told, would be instrumental to helping each other that weekend. In the process of working together, we would learn more about ourselves and how we handled the relationships in our lives. Both past and present.

The meeting room would become our playground, our stage, our refuge. It was where we'd explore the reasons we'd chosen to attend, focus on what was most important to us, and decide how we may want to approach relationships differently going forward.

I was excited to begin.

Before Friday's session came to a close, the instructors handed each of us a nine-line poem to read and think about. We'd each have a turn to present our version of it to the others the next day. My hand shot up when the instructors asked for a volunteer who'd be willing to start things off. I loved poetry. I loved presenting. And I loved being first! They chose me.

My turn on Saturday morning, however, was full of twists I never saw coming.

To begin with, the poem wasn't the rhyming kind. It wasn't even particularly eloquent. And then, instead of being asked for my interpretation of it, I discovered—as student number one—that we'd instead be breaking it down into the smallest of parts, beginning with the first word—I.

Taking my place in the center of the room, the word came out without flair.

"I."

I shrugged my shoulders and smiled with confidence, enjoying going first and being in front of a crowd. I'd always been a great student. This would be a cinch.

The male instructor paused and tilted his head to one side. "What's behind your *I*?" he asked.

"Behind my I?" I asked, confused.

Along with my fellow students, I'd discover that the tone and inflection of my voice—as well as my body language and the scenarios I set up to illustrate the words and phrases in the poem—would reveal my inner thoughts. Whether I was conscious of them or not.

Many of the words in the poem were triggers that

uncovered feelings below the surface—those we were aware of, those we didn't realize we carried around with us, and those we didn't want to admit we had. We'd discover through role-playing and deep discussions exactly what those words meant to us and how we'd chosen to treat ourselves and others based on the beliefs we'd formed at a young age.

The words by themselves were innocuous.
People. Love. Victim.
Sad. Depressed. Angry.
Always blaming others.
Stuck.
Making things happen.
Power.

"I" was just the beginning of our stories.

Since I was the first student, I had no example to follow. I didn't know what the instructor expected me to say.

What was "behind" my I?

A few pointed questions from him revealed some of my inner sadness, previous bouts of depression, and my unexpressed anger. There'd been a good bit of blaming others in my life, and I was definitely feeling stuck—and powerless—in my relationship with Charlie. Since I'd gone into the weekend expecting to get confirmation that all my neuroses stemmed from that relationship, I was stopped cold when the instructor paused the action just a few words into my turn and asked, "Who abandoned you?"

I froze.

What had I said or done—and how had I said or done it—that made him ask me this?

I wasn't attending the retreat because someone had abandoned me. I was attending because my stepfather had been a controlling and overbearing disciplinarian all my life, and I needed more tools in my toolbox to deal with him.

Who abandoned you? His question rang in my head.

There was a stillness in the air. Tears came to my eyes. And then I heard myself mumble the answer.

"My dad."

My dad's smile—that beautiful beaming smile that I'd seen on the pages of my baby book when working on the exercise for my counseling session—flashed in front of my eyes. I'd written in my journal that night that the most overwhelming feeling I had when looking through those pictures had been love. I was the first—and only—child my parents had had together, and every picture of the three of us together exuded that love.

Standing in front of my fellow students, I remembered other thoughts I'd written in my journal that night.

This overwhelming feeling of love in turn made me think of my dad. And I felt very empty. Not void of emotion, but the empty you feel when you no longer have someone who was very important to you. As if he had died.

Though I'd purposefully not tracked him down in Sheboygan the previous fall, and though I'd told myself I was done trying to keep a connection, after looking at the photos, I'd found myself writing, *I miss him. I don't understand how he could have let me go again. I want to know how he is, but I don't know why.*

That weekend, I began to understand why. He and I were inextricably connected—and the pain of being disconnected from him hurt me more than I'd wanted to admit.

But I didn't want to reach out again. Make myself vulnerable again.

Being my biological father, I reasoned he should've felt an innate longing to stay connected to me. I'd leaned on that hope but had learned not to trust it, running through the stages of grief more times than I could count.

Denial.

Anger.

Bargaining.
Depression.
Acceptance.

Over the years, we'd reconnected, and I'd think we were moving forward only to find, like a hamster on a wheel, that I was right back where I'd started from, with acceptance being more elusive each time.

"What would it be like to forgive your father and concentrate on loving yourself?" the female leader asked me later that day.

Forgive him? It seemed an impossible and unfair thing to ask me to do. *How could I? Why would I?*

Over time, and by listening to the wisdom of those around me—instructors and assistants alike—I learned some answers to those questions. How I could forgive him would take place within myself—with a shift in my perspective and a change of heart. Why I would forgive him would be for myself—to give myself peace by letting go.

I'd been fighting a battle within myself, and my inner struggle wasn't hurting my dad—it was only hurting me. Forgiving someone, I began to understand, didn't mean that what they did or said was acceptable or that it didn't matter and I should just move on. Forgiving someone was a matter of seeing that what they did was for their own reasons—because of who they were, what they'd experienced, and how they perceived the world. It was separate from me. The way my dad moved unpredictably in and out of my life had nothing to do with me.

Saturday evening, we did an exercise where we reimagined a scene from our childhood. Instead of remembering something the way it had happened, we imagined it turning out the way we wished it would have. I chose my canceled Christmas.

My dad picked me up on the day he'd said he would. He

told me that he loved me, and he explained what was happening in his life. How he was drinking too much, but he'd get help. How he'd messed up things with Sherry, but he'd try to do better. He didn't leave me hanging. And he never left my life.

I felt whole. Complete. And at peace.

By Sunday afternoon, I had many new tools in my toolbox. I'd leaned into making mistakes, feeling for the first time that it was okay to make them. It was part of the human experience, and at the Global Relationship Center, it was even applauded. I learned the difference between being "right" and being close, and that sometimes, even if you felt you were "right," being close might be more important. It was a good thought to consider. I was told, "When you know better, you do better." It was all right that I hadn't known better before. I was learning, and I could choose differently going forward.

I'd spent so many years judging myself based on the words and actions of both my dad and Charlie, as well as those of other men in my life, instead of seeing that what they did and said was all about *them*, not *me*. I now knew that I could choose how I felt about myself independent of their opinions or expectations. And it was life-changing to realize that I'd built my own belief system, and I could change it at any time.

I wasn't stuck.

I could make things happen.

I was powerful.

Like Dorothy learning that all she had to do was click her red heels together to get home, I learned I'd held the power to change my own perspective all along.

One by one, the twelve of us worked through the words and phrases in our poem. For some, it took twenty minutes. For others, it took hours. We each circled back to repeating the word "I," but with a whole lot more confidence and joy "behind" it than when we'd started.

Before the weekend was over, I decided to be kinder to Charlie when he and my mom visited. I would treat him like I'd treat any other guest in my home rather than avoiding him, as I often had. But I'd also keep my boundaries intact and stand up for myself. He was just a guy, I realized, a human being. He had limited tools like the rest of us.

Like my dad.

It would take me longer to see him that way. To understand —without sadness or anger or expectation—that he was also simply human. I'd expected more from him.

If I didn't want to experience another cycle of hope, disappointment, and grief, I finally realized, I could choose to see that him "being a dad," with all the expectations and responsibilities that that entailed, was not part of his makeup. I could choose not to expect him to fill that role, not in a passive-aggressive way, but with true acceptance.

Recognizing that he was who he was and that he would do what he would do—and that it had nothing to do with me— gave me freedom from the pain that my unmet expectations had continually caused.

Once I accepted that and felt I could live with it, I could forgive him. And forgiveness was a gift for both of us. It meant I could love him again with my whole heart. And I did.

Sunday evening, before we wrapped up our course activities, I began my journey back to him once again. Not with complete forgiveness yet, but with an open heart. And a yearning to reach out in spite of what may come.

Upon my request to make a phone call, an instructor led me to a quiet front office, tucked away from the volunteers and other students. I dialed Grandma Wilsing's number, memorized from childhood, from the rotary phone on the desk. I had no idea if he would answer.

He did.

And the wheel, once again, began to turn.

CHAPTER 20
A Clipping in My Wallet

FEBRUARY 1995

Dear Bessers, my dad's letter to me began. We'd been writing to each other for nearly a year, and now, every letter I received made me happy. It was wonderful to be connected again, even in a long-distance, occasional way. My dad was still living in Sheboygan and still installing floors for a living. I was still in Tallahassee. Larry and I were renting an apartment, and we both worked at the local newspaper.

I'm writing slow, my dad wrote to me that February, *because I know you don't teach anymore and maybe you forgot how to read fast (haha).* He couldn't help but kid around. It made me smile.

It's nice writing to you, he continued. *I always wanted to know what you were doing. I don't know if it means much but I sure am proud of you—how you got to be who you are.*

That made me pause. It was so nice to know he felt that way.

Remember how for some reason you thought I was not the way you wanted me to be? Well, I had a lot of problems then—bills and wives.

You know. I always carry a clipping in my wallet. You must have maybe saw it somewhere printed but it goes like this:

> <u>Accept Me</u>
> *You say I wouldn't do that if I were you*
> *And all I can say is, oh, yes, you would too*
> *'Cause if you were me, you'd be me inside*
> *You'd have all my feelings, my hurt, and my pride*
> *You'd do what I do, and you'd say what I say*
> *'Cause if you were me, you'd be me all the way*
> *And if I were you, it would be the same deal*
> *I'd be you all over, forever, for real*
> *But the fact of the matter is easy to see*
> *What you want to do is be you inside me*

It was as if my dad had reached through the letter and grabbed my heart. I reread it, taking in every word. Had he been a poet, I could've imagined him writing it. He'd likely felt this way for years, and I wondered how long he'd been carrying the clipping in his wallet. And why he hadn't sent it sooner—right after the retreat, after we'd talked. Maybe the universe had known that I needed more time.

After my initial retreat weekend, I'd returned to the center almost monthly to assist others. Each time, I learned more about the power of forgiveness, love, and acceptance—not only in relation to others but in the way I treated myself. I gained insight from each student who took their turn, from the other assistants who shared their stories, and from the instructors who gently guided us along. And as I put more of what I was learning into practice, I shared my new understanding with others.

The poem my dad sent arrived ten months after that first weekend. Perhaps providence stepped in when I was ready to receive his message.

In the same letter in which he'd sent the poem, he commented on a newspaper article I'd sent to him. I'd recently acted in a community play, and a picture of me on stage appeared with the review. He said I looked tall.

How tall are you? he wrote. It struck me that he didn't know. He hadn't seen me in almost ten years, not since I was eighteen and he'd said goodbye to me at Grandma's house before I moved to Florida.

I was never in a play, he went on, *but I once had my leg in a cast. Old joke.*

He mentioned that Cliff had just turned seventeen.

I can't wait, he wrote. *One more year and I can see Cliff without Debra saying I'm breaking the law. Just think, someday I'll have two sons back. That's going to be something else.*

He was so excited, and he was so close.

He wrote about Cliff again in a letter he sent that December, just a month before Cliff's eighteenth birthday.

Well, January 25, maybe I can see Cliff—if he wants to. I don't know. It's been so long. I don't even know how to go about it. Do you? Give me a hint, please. Or should I just wait till Clint's eighteen and see them both at once? I don't know. You're the brain—tell me. You know Debra.

I'm sure I encouraged him. At some point, I'd let him know I'd met the boys, and I'd been corresponding with each of them by letter as well. I knew they wanted to meet our dad.

Two months later, in February 1996, he sent an update.

Last Saturday, there was a knock on my door.

That Saturday had been nine days after Cliff's birthday. I held my breath and kept reading, hoping for the best.

There was a guy on each side and a girl in the middle. The guy on the left said, "I'm Cliff and that's Clint, and this is my girlfriend." I looked for a second and said, "Wow!!!" and we all hugged each other.

Was that great! I couldn't believe it. Still can't.

The thought of the three of them reuniting filled me with

joy. My dad got to hug his boys. The boys got to hug their dad. I hoped it would be the beginning of something wonderful for all of them. For all of us.

Dad said that Cliff shared a bit about his and Clint's past, relaying that they'd gotten into trouble with the law starting in their early teens, before Larry and I had even met them. And he shared that he and his girlfriend, Erin, were getting married soon.

I'm glad with all that's happened with them that they turned out pretty damn good, Dad wrote. I wondered how much Cliff had told him. He'd shared some of their past with me, but I was sure I didn't know everything either.

They both were very nice guys, he wrote, obviously proud of the boys who were his sons. *They were cool looking.*

That made me laugh. So did Dad's take on Clint.

He don't talk a lot. I think Cliff's in charge of him.

From the little I'd been with the boys, I'd thought the same thing.

At the end of the letter, he wrote:

I wish I could see you once, but I guess you never get back here. There's maybe no reason for you to come because you seem to have your life together down there. Oh well, maybe someday before I'm 100, like George Burns, I'll get to see you, My little Bessers.

He wished me luck in the new house I'd purchased. I'd mentioned it to Cliff in a recent letter, and I guess Cliff had told him. Funny to think my dad was learning information about me from him.

May God bless it, he closed with. *Take care & write soon. Love DAD.*

I didn't know when I'd be traveling to Wisconsin next, but I expected that when I did, I'd visit Tara, both of my brothers, and our dad. Almost everyone was reconnected.

CHAPTER 21
The Trouble with the Law

FALL 1996

So much of life comes down to timing. As it turned out, the invitation for my ten-year high-school reunion in Sheboygan came just a few months after the reunion of my brothers and our dad. It was planned for September, and Larry and I made arrangements to go. We hoped to see everyone—Sherry and Tara, Cliff and Clint, and my dad.

In the three years since I'd reunited with Cliff and Clint, we'd stayed in touch as best we could. The trouble with the law Cliff had mentioned to our dad had begun for them at the ages of ten and eleven, and by their mid-teens included everything from vandalism to drugs to grand theft. At fourteen and fifteen, shortly after our first visit in 1993, they'd been assigned to separate juvenile detention centers in Wisconsin.

Cliff shared in later years that he'd started running away from home when he was eleven, shortly after he and Clint had moved with their mother, Debra, and their adoptive father, Mike, from the outskirts of town into the city of Manitowoc.

Mike had been abusive and even though he wasn't around much once they moved, home life was still chaotic. The boys preferred to be anywhere but there.

"Clint and I basically lived in the streets, stayed with friends, slept wherever we could," he told me.

Debra divorced Mike that year and married her third husband a couple years later when the boys were twelve and thirteen. "He was a good guy," Cliff said, "but by that time, I'd already developed a fuck-you attitude toward authority."

He'd celebrated his thirteenth birthday while living in a group home. "It was great though," he said. "They had pool tables and video games." Having to live there did not serve as a deterrent for him. It was more of a vacation in a luxury home.

At a young age, Clint had also felt that consequences of crime weren't so bad. One of his brother Cliff's first escapades had resulted in him having to do community service, so he volunteered at a local food pantry where the boys were allowed to choose from items that were left at the end of each day.

"We loaded up on free candy and snacks," Clint said. "It was great."

When they'd gone to separate facilities in 1993, Clint had been a sophomore in high school. He was sent to Rawhide, a boys ranch for at-risk and delinquent youth, an hour and a half from Manitowoc.

He wrote to me from there and, in one of his letters, included a picture he'd taken at a recent Green Bay Packers' game at Lambeau Field. It was signed, *To Gina, Best Wishes—Bart Starr*.

Starr was a legendary NFL champion and a co-founder of Rawhide. He made regular appearances there to talk with and encourage the boys, and the boys had been able to attend a game while staying at the facility.

I had him sign it for you, Clint wrote. *I never told you about it before cause I wanted it to be a surprise. So, SURPRISE!"*

It touched my heart that this teenage boy, a super sports fan who loved the Packers and loved football, had wanted to share this with me. He included a second picture, one of himself. On the back, in perfect cursive, he wrote, *To Gina with Love from Clint, xxxooo. I've been saying my prayers.*

He did well at Rawhide. He got recognized as a Student of the Month and stayed clean for more than a year.

His junior year, he was back at his high school and living at home with Debra and her third husband.

But by the time Larry and I arrived in the fall of 1996, he was at the Manitowoc County Jail, on a work-release schedule so he could attend classes during his senior year. We had to squeeze in time with him after class let out and before he needed to report back to the jail, so we met outside the school grounds in the parking lot of a gas station for a little less than an hour.

Cliff was also in a work-release program through the jail at that time, and we met him and his girlfriend, Erin, in a parking lot outside of the place where he was working.

Cliff had dropped out of school as a high-school sophomore and earned his high-school equivalency degree the following year while living at Lincoln Hills School, a juvenile correctional facility. When he returned to Manitowoc at the age of seventeen, he reunited with Erin, who he'd known for several years.

They were planning to get married soon, Cliff told us the day Larry and I met them in the parking lot. I remembered our dad writing to me about that. It was hard to know what to say. I was happy they had each other, but they were so young. Erin introduced us to her one-year old, her daughter from a previous relationship.

There was so much to take in.

For starters, it was hard to wrap my mind around having a baby at seventeen. I'd been so determined to not get pregnant in high school—mostly for fear of what Charlie would think of me—that I hadn't had sex until college. And I couldn't imagine getting married at eighteen. Larry and I'd been engaged for just a few months and were planning our wedding for the following spring. We were in our late twenties, busy in our careers in journalism, and we were looking to buy our first house. Children hadn't entered the picture yet and still seemed a long way off. I couldn't relate.

Larry and I also had never had an entanglement with the law—except for my one tiny episode of shoplifting during seventh grade when I'd pinched a strawberry Bonnie Belle lip gloss and stick of beef jerky from the local *Park & Shop*. Fellow classmates looked on as my two closest friends and I got handcuffed and carted away in the back of a cop car. That and getting picked up by our parents at the police station had been the only deterrent I'd needed.

Cliff and Clint had never physically hurt anyone, but theft, vandalism, and drugs were areas way out of my comfort zone—as was having to meet a loved one on the sly because they were serving time at the county jail.

And yet, we were connected. We were family. I'd spent so many years thinking about them, now that I'd finally reunited with them, I wanted them to stay in my life.

In each letter I wrote back to them, I encouraged them to stay on a straight path. In an effort to better understand their world, I learned more about juvenile delinquency and recidivism. I became a mentor with the Juvenile Justice system in Tallahassee and later became a Big Sister with Big Brothers Big Sisters of America. I couldn't be there for my brothers when they were growing up, but knowing what they'd experienced in their youth inspired me to help the children I could.

Though my visits with Cliff and Clint had been short, I was grateful we'd been able to see each other again. I hoped our next visits would be under better circumstances. That they'd be free of their current lifestyle and that this would be the last time either of them would be incarcerated. One day soon, I hoped to receive letters from them with a return address of a home, not an institution.

CHAPTER 22
His Family Photo Album

FALL 1996

My dad knew Larry and I were coming to Wisconsin for a long weekend. He knew we'd go to Manitowoc first to meet with Cliff and Clint and then visit him in Sheboygan. The festivities for my ten-year high-school reunion would start Friday evening with a gathering at a local bar. We'd see my dad Friday afternoon before going out. It would be our ten-year reunion as well, and Larry would meet my dad for the first time.

Though my dad and I had been writing to each other for two years—ever since the Sunday evening I'd called him from my first weekend retreat—the idea of seeing him in person made me nervous. The last time I'd seen him, which had been at Grandma's house after my lunch with her, I'd been so angry with him. All I'd wanted back then was an apology, and he hadn't given me one.

Things were different now.

For starters, this visit had been my choice, and I now had a new perspective. It was a huge shift from my thoughts and feelings a decade earlier. I'd learned to lay my expectations aside, hoping he'd stay in touch but knowing he might not. I was delighted that he had.

But my anxiety grew as Larry and I rounded the corner onto North Fourth Street, the last address my dad had written from. I went from being uneasy about seeing him after so much time to wondering if he'd even be there. Was this really going to happen? Or would we find no one there?

Larry parked on the street in front of the house with the correct address. Though I knew we were only a mile from Grandma's, it felt worlds away. Everything around us was unfamiliar to me.

"You okay?" Larry reached out his hand. I took it and squeezed, and then took a deep breath.

"Yeah." I felt too on edge to smile, but I was happy we were there.

On the drive over, I'd tried to picture being with my dad again. I'd envisioned the dad from my childhood—the one who'd taught me to play guitar and had let me sing into his real microphone. I'd pictured his smiling eyes and his blonde hair and thought of how he'd tickled my knee to make me laugh. He'd made me feel safe, and most of all, loved. I'd missed that dad so much.

I stepped out of the car and looked up. He was just coming out of the house.

He didn't look like the dad I'd envisioned.

He looked pale, and his hair was a darker shade of blonde than I remembered. He looked much older than his fifty-two years. He wore a loose red t-shirt, emblazoned with "Down by the Old Millstream" in huge white letters across his chest. I noticed a small hole near the bottom hem. My eyes went from the hole to the baggy beige khakis he wore that looked a size too big.

Feeling overdressed—I wasn't but in comparison felt like I

was—I buttoned up my plaid flannel shirt over my black turtleneck and belted blue jeans. I looked down at my leather shoes, wishing I hadn't worn them. I remembered feeling self-conscious of my clothing as a child, being careful to not wear anything too nice to Grandma's for fear of making her or my dad feel inferior.

I closed the car door and stepped up the walkway to meet him halfway.

I'd wanted this moment so badly. I'd waited for it. And finally, it was here.

My dad smiled a wide smile.

"You look like a movie star!" he announced before I got all the way to him. He threw his arms up in the air as if introducing me to the neighborhood.

We embraced, and I kissed him on the cheek.

I introduced him to Larry, they shook hands, and he invited us in for a drink.

"I've been here a few months." He led us up a steep staircase to the second floor. "A buddy of mine lives downstairs and lets me stay up here."

He opened the door to a room that reminded me of the attic at Grandma's, sparsely decorated but tidy. My eyes scanned the place for guitars, amps, a microphone stand—anything familiar, anything reminiscent of what had once been, of who he had once been. I saw none of that, only a simple tan sofa and worn wooden coffee table. Another table sat in the kitchenette, a 1960's-style aluminum one surrounded by aluminum chairs with bright yellow padding. The whole setup looked like something out of the seventies.

My dad motioned for Larry and me to have a seat on the couch. He grabbed three cans of Pabst Blue Ribbon from the refrigerator, handed one to each of us, and then pulled a kitchen chair into the living room to sit near us.

We sat. We drank. We made small talk.

This used to be so easy, I thought. Now there was just empty space and awkward silence.

Are you there, Dad? I wanted to whisper. *It's me—Bessers.*

But something felt off.

We continued to sit and sip, with my dad and I looking at each other like we were trying to remember and trying to forget at the same time.

"I saw your engagement announcement," he said finally. He looked at me expectantly.

My stomach tightened. I hadn't listed him as one of my parents. I was hoping he hadn't seen it.

I sat up straighter and looked at Larry to steady myself. Our engagement announcement had run in *The Sheboygan Press*, my hometown paper, about a month before.

Gina Beth Wilsing and Lawrence Mitchell Davidson, Jr., both of Tallahassee, Florida, are engaged to be married, it read. *Their parents are...*

I remembered my fingers clicking the keys as I'd typed it and how I'd paused when I'd gotten to that part.

Their parents are...

The word itself technically qualified my dad, but when I'd thought of listing his name, it had felt unjust. Even though he was currently part of my life, he'd stepped out again and again. He hadn't done the work. Even though I'd come to terms with who he was and what I could and could not expect from him, and I'd realized that forgiving him was best for both of us, that only got him so far.

My mom and Charlie had parented me—for better or for worse, in sickness and in health. And though Charlie had gone at it like it was a business deal, he'd at least put in the hours. He'd worked overtime. He'd taught me all sorts of important and practical things that dads teach daughters—how to drive a car, how to buy a car, how to budget, how to fix things around the house. In the few years between my weekend retreat and my engagement, Charlie had even mellowed a bit. I guess I had, too.

Most importantly, despite our ups and downs, Charlie had never quit. He'd never walked away. So, he'd be the one walking me down the aisle. And he was the one listed as my parent on my engagement announcement. To have listed my dad, as if he were an equal parent, would have been a slight to the man who'd raised me.

Had my dad been reading the paper and come across our announcement? Or had someone shown it to him?

I'd known it might be hard for him to take if he saw it, but I'd hoped he'd understand, that he'd be able to see where I was coming from. But I could tell by the dejected look on his face that he didn't. To him—no matter what—he was still my dad.

As if on cue, he shrugged and said, "I'm just your father." Then he tilted his head back and laughed his easy laugh, the way he used to when he'd had too much to drink and he'd tell me how the world had wronged him.

His reaction didn't sway my resolve. It just made me sad for him. I'd already wrestled with these thoughts and feelings, and even face-to-face, I stood by my decision. It had been the right one, even if it broke his heart.

Seconds later, his demeanor flipped. His eyes lit up, and he pulled out a large book from under an end table.

"Oh, I have something to show you," he said brightly. "It's my family photo album."

He handed me the album. Proudly, like a child sharing his most prized possession. I laid it on my lap and scooted closer to Larry before lifting its cover, expecting to see old pictures of Grandma and Grandpa and my dad's three older brothers. To my surprise, behind the glossy cellophane on the first page, I saw my younger self smiling. I glanced up at my dad, whose eyes were fixed on me. It never occurred to me that he had any pictures of me.

Larry sipped his beer and remained focused on the photos, unaware of the emotional significance of the moment.

I began flipping through the pages, finding myself in picture after picture—riding on my dad's shoulders, picnicking with him at a city park, water-skiing at my aunt's lake house. There were pictures of me and my dad laughing together, making silly faces, sitting side by side on the couch. There were pictures from the Christmases and birthdays we'd celebrated together.

Continuing on, I found photos of Cliff and Clint. First, as babies, then as toddlers. I recognized a Polaroid picture from my last Christmas with them. I had a similar one in an album of my own. The boys were dressed in their red footie-pajamas, and we were gathered around our dad on his living room couch.

I paused, thinking about how different it felt to sit on his living room couch now. How detached I felt though all I'd wanted to feel was connected. I looked at the little boys in that photo and thought of how many years had passed since then. How much of their lives we'd missed and how grateful I was to know them now.

Turning the page, I came across our sister—baby Tara—wrapped in her blanket, sleeping in her crib, learning to walk. Her white-blond hair sprouting out like duck down, her blue eyes shining.

There were no pictures of my mom. Or of Cliff's and Clint's mom, or of Tara's.

Just us—his four children—while we'd been a part of his life. Using our pictures, he'd pieced together what he hadn't been able to hold onto for long: a family of his own.

His family photo album.

In reality, we were the children he'd loved and then let go. Yet the photo album was telling me that maybe he never really did let go. Maybe he'd held on in ways we never knew—held on in his heart. To him, the four of us would always be his family.

I flipped through the empty pages at the back of the book, and a commencement program from my high-school graduation fell out. My eyes followed it to the floor. I'd forgotten he'd gone. Though he'd tried to tell me, back at Grandma's the last time I'd seen him, I hadn't been interested in anything he'd had to say.

He picked the program up and set it on the table.

"I saw you, but you didn't see me," he said, turning to me. This time, I was listening. "I took Grandma. I was real proud of you that day."

I thought about them looking down on my graduation ceremony from the top of Vollrath Bowl, the city park where ceremonies had been held for decades. I imagined them hearing my name and watching me walk across the stage to get my diploma. Had he wanted to reach out? To let me know he was proud of me? Had Grandma? I was touched that they'd come. Back then, it would've just upset me to know it. Now, I was grateful to know they'd come in spite of our separation.

I closed the album and rested it beside the program on the table. Larry rose to set his empty beer can on the kitchen counter, and my dad and I followed suit, breaking the silence with idle chit chat.

"My classmates are meeting soon," I said. I felt restless and ready to go.

So many feelings swirled within me—sadness that he'd missed so many milestones in my life and confusion about how to move forward. Even now that we'd seen each other, he wouldn't be coming to my wedding. I didn't even know if I'd invite him. After not being in my engagement announcement, wouldn't it just hurt him more to receive an invitation, knowing he wouldn't be able to attend? He didn't have the resources to come to Florida, and even if he'd been able to snap his fingers and be there, he wouldn't have fit in. He wasn't part of that world. My world. He'd long ago separated himself from it, and there was no bringing him back.

"Yeah," Larry said, coming to my aid. "I guess it's time for us to go get ready."

My dad nodded and led us back downstairs to the front door. We walked out into the cool air coming off Lake Michigan, and Larry suggested taking a picture of the two of us to commemorate our reunion. My dad put his arm around me, and we smiled for the camera—me in my turtleneck and blue jeans, and my dad in his red t-shirt and bell-bottoms. Standing side-by-side, our physical similarities were evident. We were unmistakably father and daughter. What was not clear, however, was how to carry out those roles in each other's lives.

That December, I sent my dad a Christmas card—to the same address where Larry and I had visited with him just a few months earlier. It came back stamped, *Return to Sender. Address Unknown.*

I never heard from him again.

Part Four

CHAPTER 23
Overlapping Lines

JUNE 1998

Cliff, Clint, and I exchanged letters for nearly two years following my reunion trip to Wisconsin. During that time, Larry and I got married, moved to Charlotte, North Carolina, and bought a house. Clint finished his senior year and graduated from high school without incident. And Cliff and Erin had a baby.

Cliff had remained incarcerated for nearly a year after we left, and Erin had visited him regularly. She'd called me early on in her pregnancy to tell me the news and to let me know she was thinking about going back to work as a dancer. She'd already called the employer to get details.

"The place is really classy," she said. "And right here in town."

In town meant in Manitowoc. She was living in a trailer home, had custody of her daughter, and now a baby on the way. With Cliff in jail, their financial needs fell on her.

"I'd make a hundred and twenty dollars an hour, and I'd get to keep sixty."

My heart ached for her, but at the same time, I saw the hole she'd dug for herself. They'd dug for themselves. And it just kept getting deeper and deeper.

Erin called me often during the months Cliff was in jail, and while I was happy to have another link to my brother and be Erin's "big sister" as well, I was afraid that if I got too involved, their problems would somehow become mine. Giving too much, or offering to help, might cause them to lean on me more than I was comfortable with. All the miles between Wisconsin and North Carolina made it easier. I was safe in my bubble in Charlotte, available only by phone or through letters.

Cliff was released from jail a couple of months before the birth of their son in November 1997.

Three months later, Erin was pregnant again.

The last I'd heard—before answering a knock on my door at five o'clock one summer morning—was that Erin was due that November, and Cliff was on probation.

Larry and I worked nights at the newspaper and often got home around two a.m., so it wasn't unusual for us to be up in the wee hours of the morning. That particular morning, we'd been walking up the stairs to go to bed when the knock came, startling both of us.

Our eyes locked, and we padded toward the foyer. With one finger, I inched aside a curtain to peek out the window and saw the silhouettes of a man and a woman against the first rays of dawn.

"Gina." The deep voice came from outside. "It's Cliff."

My mouth dropped. *What the hell?* Larry looked at me, bewildered.

What were they doing here?

I took a breath to settle myself and slowly opened the door. I stepped out to hug Cliff, and the woman with him came into view.

She was not Erin.

All I could do was stare.

She gave me a sheepish grin, then looked down, letting her long white-blonde bangs cover most of her face. My disbelieving eyes went from her to him.

"What are you doing here?" I couldn't imagine there was anything he could say that would make sense.

Cliff shuffled his feet. "Jamie has an aunt and uncle here. And you're here. So, we decided to visit." He said it as though it was perfectly reasonable, but his eyes didn't meet mine.

I was speechless. And unsure of what to do next.

He was here, at my home. I loved him, but could I trust him?

And who was she?

And where was Erin—pregnant Erin—and their baby boy?

"Come in," I found myself saying. I motioned toward the open door. Larry was standing in the foyer. Cliff and Jamie said hello and stepped past him. Larry looked at me with questions in his eyes that I didn't have answers to.

What the hell?

I was sure we were both thinking it.

We ushered Cliff and Jamie to the couches in our living room, and they sat side-by-side.

We wanted answers.

"We had to get away," Cliff explained. "Erin is crazy. She called the cops. She told them I hit her—I didn't."

This was what I'd been afraid of. Being leaned on too much. Getting involved.

She called the cops and said you hit her? And now you're here with some girl we don't even know—some girl who's not your pregnant wife?

"We drove through the night," Cliff said. "I had to leave."

Remembering he was on probation raised new concerns. I wasn't fully informed about the rules of probation, but I knew you needed to be on your best behavior and was pretty sure you couldn't just leave town.

Were the cops searching for him? Would he get arrested if he was found? Did this mean Larry and I were harboring a fugitive?

The lines of our lives were overlapping in exactly the ways I'd been trying to avoid. It turned out the distance between Wisconsin and North Carolina wasn't so far after all.

Larry went to the kitchen to get Cliff and Jamie some water, and I tried to clear my head of the conflicting thoughts within it. Although Cliff had shown up under less than desirable circumstances, I didn't know if he'd ever be here again, so I decided to make the most of it.

Like my dad, I also had a family photo album containing pictures from our younger years, back when we were a family —a family that he had no memories of. I laid it on Cliff's lap and watched him flip the pages like my dad had watched me. It was a way to let Cliff know he was important to me. That he'd always been important to me, from the time he was born. That's how I'd felt looking through my dad's album.

Larry returned with the water, and the four of us talked for a while, as if we were just old friends catching up. As if we'd expected them to arrive. As if the sun wasn't rising, and we didn't have to work the next day. But we did have to. In fact, Larry was scheduled to go in early the next day. And now we had near-strangers in our home, who we didn't entirely trust, but who obviously needed a place to sleep.

"Would you like to stay in our guest room?" I asked. Larry gave me a subtle glance, and I knew he was thinking the same thing I was.

Are they going to rob us blind while we sleep?

The moment after I thought it, I felt guilty for thinking it.

Cliff was my brother, right? He was still the child I'd loved, the one I'd held in the Christmas pictures we'd just looked at. He was still the teenage boy I'd held in my heart and had found after more than a dozen years of hoping I would. We'd written each other letters, and I'd visited him twice. He trusted me.

But could we trust him?

He was an adult now, and one who'd made poor choices. In fact, he'd made several in the last twenty-four hours. In plain language, he was a thief and a drug dealer. He was a felon. He'd spent time in prison. Would my thin relationship with him really stop him and this girl from stealing possessions they could sell on the streets for the cash they may need? For drugs they might do? We'd never even met her before. What had she done in the past?

Was I terrible for thinking these thoughts, or was I stupid for taking them in?

"If that would be okay," Cliff said.

Jamie half-smiled and tucked her long locks behind her ears.

I hugged Cliff goodnight, said goodnight to her, and let Larry lead them upstairs. I hid everything I considered to be valuable.

A few hours after going to bed, around nine that morning, I awoke and called my manager at the paper to get the day off. I wasn't going to wake up Cliff and Jamie and tell them to leave. And I wasn't going to leave them alone in our house.

Larry left for work around ten, and I waited while they slept, a stream of thoughts going through my mind. Would they ask to stay another night? Would they want something from me, like money? Was I safe to be alone with them?

They woke up shortly after Larry left and didn't ask for a thing. Not even breakfast. They seemed happy to be on their way, headed to Jamie's aunt and uncle. I wondered if they'd let them know they were coming.

I hugged Cliff and wished him well, and said goodbye to Jamie, still having no idea what part she played in all this.

After they left, I felt bad that I'd judged them so harshly. It was true he had broken probation. And Erin had called the cops and accused him of hitting her. And he had traveled across the country with this Jamie girl. But after all our worry about Cliff and Jamie taking advantage of us, there had been nothing to worry about.

Then the phone calls came.

First, from Erin.

"Did he come by you?" I could hear her rage. "Was he with *that girl?*" I could feel the heat of her anger through the phone. "He hit me, you know. I called the cops. That's why he left. Do you know where they are?"

Yes, I told her, he'd been at our house, and yes, he was with that girl. Maybe I even told her where they were heading. I had no reason not to. But my fears about getting too close were making my insides turn over. I was smack in the middle of this episode in their lives, and I didn't want to be.

"Let me know if you hear from him, okay?"

I told her I would, though I wasn't expecting him to come back.

We hung up, and within minutes, Clint called, equally enraged, but in defense of his brother.

"Why did you tell Erin that Cliff was there? You have no idea what she's like!"

I'd never heard him raise his voice before. And he was right. I didn't know what she was like in regard to this. Or what Cliff was like. I didn't know what had actually happened and had no experience with domestic violence or probation. I'd never known anyone who had these issues.

Feeling way too close to their chaos, and not knowing how to navigate these strange waters, I chose to opt out.

Erin shouldn't be calling me in a panic to find her husband. Clint shouldn't be judging my actions, telling me who I could speak to and what I could say. I wanted no part of that.

"Call me back when y'all have your shit together," I told Clint. It was harsh, but I was done for now.

He must have relayed the message to Cliff and Erin because Erin never called again, and Cliff didn't write.

Five months later, in early December, I broke the silence I'd demanded.

Do you want to be right, or do you want to be close? The words from the Understanding Yourself and Others course reverberated in my head. *Was I right?* I didn't even know. *But did I want to be close?* Yes. I knew that for sure.

In a letter to Cliff that December, I told him I loved him no matter what but, looking to maintain my boundaries, I also told him how it had felt to have him just show up—after breaking probation, fleeing the cops, and leaving his pregnant wife—with some girl we didn't know. I'd wanted him to understand the impact of his actions.

I reiterated what I'd said to Clint over the phone back in June, but in slightly softer terms.

Send me some good news when you have some, I'd written. *Stay out of trouble. Write to me when all this crap is behind you.*

The following week, I received Cliff's reply letter. The envelope had the return address of the Dodge Correctional Institution in Waupun, Wisconsin. Stamped in large, black, capital letters were the words, *FROM THE WISCONSIN PRISON SYSTEM.*

I assumed it was not good news.

CHAPTER 24
Closer Than That

DECEMBER 1998

The envelope felt heavy in my hand. I looked at the big block letters that told me Cliff was likely behind bars once again. And that he was back in Wisconsin. Either he'd gone willingly or he'd been found.

I hoped his incarceration had come after the birth of his second child, who'd been due in November, so that he'd been able to be there. That is if he and Erin were speaking. She hadn't contacted me since June.

Sitting in the same spot on our sofa where Cliff and Jamie had sat on the night they'd arrived, I opened the envelope and began to read.

I would like to apologize for my self-centered and unannounced appearance at your house, his letter began.

Relief washed over me. It was a good start.

I didn't see it as being a "problem" for you. I was wrong. I thought my visit would have been a good thing, a "pleasant surprise" more so. I meant no harm or disrespect.

Despite his immaturity at thinking his visit could've been a nice surprise, I was grateful to get an explanation. I relaxed into the sofa cushions, ready to read more.

I always thought of you as a "mentor" or my support. Somebody I could turn to when I <u>needed</u> it.

Noting the word was underlined, I paused, thinking of how desperate he must have felt. He'd turned to me, and I'd taken him in but then pushed him away the very next day.

I had gone through hell this summer. I turned to everybody that normally helped me, but Erin had been quick to make shit up and put me in the wrong, which drew sympathy to her and left me very alone, confused, and hopeless. When all else failed, I thought of you. Somebody who was independent, strong-willed, loved me, and I figured would help me no matter what the situation. Plus you were hours away so I could be at peace.

He'd shared none of those deeper feelings with me the night they'd arrived. Our meeting had been so awkward. If he had let me know they were coming, my reaction might have been different.

All I had was your address, he continued. *We couldn't find your number.*

It was at least good to know he'd tried.

Anyways, my intent was to get help and advice. I thought it was the best option I had. Sorry it caused a serious problem in our relationship.

I cocked my head at that. Was he trying to make me feel guilty?

Had I overreacted?

My relationship with both Cliff and Clint had been so fragile already. We hardly knew each other. We'd spent so little time together. Had I been the one who'd caused irreparable damage?

Cliff went on to say that I shouldn't trust Erin. That I'd have to know the truth to determine who to trust.

And as to your comment that you don't want to hear from me until

I've straightened my life out, he wrote, *if you really loved, cared, and hoped to make a difference in my life, it would mean that you'd be there in good times and bad, not just when it's convenient. It hurts to hear you say that. I thought we were a little closer than that.*

His words stung. Just as mine had stung him.

Sorry to be such a disappointment in your life. I hope that someday, somehow, we can have a close and loving relationship. You mean a lot to me, and I do, and will always love you.

It wasn't until I exhaled that I realized I'd been holding my breath. He had hope that we could be close in the future. That gave me hope as well.

Well, until I meet your standards . . .

And then there was that. I closed my eyes and shook my head. He was still a young boy—just twenty years old. Still learning. Still growing. But he cared, and he'd written back. He'd chosen to stay connected. It was enough for now.

Take care, God Bless, and best of luck to you and Larry. Happy Holidays. With love . . .

For good measure, he added a postscript.

I never asked for you to wallow in pity for me. All I asked is that I could turn to you for help, which in all reality, I never asked for. You offered it. Thank you for all you have done. It means a lot. Whether I told you or not.

I sat a long while on our couch, rereading his letter and trying to see things from his perspective. What he'd said was true. My love for him and Clint shouldn't have conditions, but my concerns were justified too. I didn't want to be entangled in their messes, and it was in my and Larry's best interest to maintain boundaries.

Cliff was right. But so was I. And we both wanted to be close.

How could we make that happen?

I wrote back to him, as the loving sister I wanted to be. It was a start.

He was incarcerated, so there was no longer a need to worry that he'd show up on my doorstep. But more than that, I wanted to be available to him. To offer advice. Or just to listen. I hoped to help him, in some small way, to turn his life around.

He'd been sentenced to three years in jail shortly after his return to Wisconsin, he told me. He'd been in Charlotte for just two days and had returned to Erin after feeling he had no other options. A couple of months later, he was taken in on previous charges.

During the two-and-a-half years he was behind bars, we exchanged monthly letters. Cliff shared the details of his life as he transferred from institution to institution, moving as he aged out of certain programs. He wrote to me about the college-level classes he was taking and about the various jobs he had within the facility. He worked as a cook—fun but hot, he said—and switched to the yard crew. *Get outside more this way*, he wrote.

I shared details of my life. I was tutoring children in reading and writing. I was a designer at the newspaper. And then, when I got pregnant in the summer of 1999, I shared how excited Larry and I were about every little thing as our baby's due date drew nearer and nearer. When Ty was born in the spring of 2000, I sent Cliff pictures of him, and Cliff in turn, sent pictures of his children to me. His son was two, and his daughter was one. He missed them terribly, he said, and he hoped to get out before Christmas that year. He was concerned though about his future with Erin.

She was doing drugs, he said, and the children had recently been placed in foster care. A routine check on their home by the Department of Children and Families had revealed signs of neglect. Erin's mother was trying to get temporary custody.

Pray 4 us? he wrote.

He shared concepts he was learning in his psychology class.

They were reminiscent of the Understanding Yourself and Others course I'd taken, and I was so grateful that he was immersing himself in the material.

My train of thought began a long time ago, he wrote, *and we all react/act different due to life experience.*

I've learned how this cycle can be passed down and down—until a change is made. That change needs to be made by me, for me and my children.

He was twenty-one when he wrote that. He still had his whole life ahead of him. A different kind of life, I hoped.

I know I've made a lot of false promises for myself in the past. But now I have time to think and plan. I have kids that need me, and if I'm not there, all I'm doing is repeating what happened to me. I won't do that to my kids anymore. It's not worth it.

I wanted to jump through my reply letter and hug him.

He shared his plan for the future with me.

I know what I need to do. Get a job. Move. And go slowly. No more living-4-the-moment type shit.

I hadn't made all the best choices in my life either and getting a different job had been the beginning of my own road to recovery. I'd moved, too. And I'd taken things slowly as well, learning that life was better when I stopped living for the moment. Different scenarios but the same idea. He seemed to have turned a corner, and I was thrilled for him.

He got certified as a reading and writing tutor for adult learners and enrolled in a horticulture class. But things with Erin had taken a drastic turn. She'd overdosed on coke, he said. She was going to go to rehab, and she wanted a divorce.

This is really not the life for me, he wrote. *Can't believe how blind I was to all of this for so long.*

I sent him one of my favorite books, *Life 101: Everything We Wish We had Learned about Life in School—but Didn't.* It had helped me put things in perspective when I was in my twenties. I hoped he would find it useful and entertaining, and that it would reinforce his determination to succeed once he was free again. As his time in prison was drawing to a close, I asked him if he truly believed his life would be different going forward.

I look at it like this. I'll be leaving this place with nothing. No money. No clothes. Not too much of anything at all. So I find it easy to fail, but I also know if I fail, I'll have to do at least six more years. That's reason enough to live like a bum for a while . . . I know I can overcome any obstacle that gets in my way. It's a matter of how bad I want to.

I have my children, whose lives I've missed so much of, and that eats at me every day. I don't want to make them, or my family and loved ones, suffer any more. It won't be easy, but it also won't be impossible. So my honest answer is yes, I truly believe I'll make it out there—legit.

I had such hope for him.

Cliff got out in November of 2000, on his son's third birthday. Previous to his release, Erin had changed her mind about their marriage. She wanted to work things out, he said, but he'd made the decision to live drug-free, and she wasn't there yet. He couldn't move back in with her. They would divorce within a year.

His mother, Debra, had moved out-of-state, and Clint was doing time, Cliff told me, but he found refuge in the home of a friend. He'd met Sarah, a girl of about twenty, shortly before going to prison. She had stayed in touch with him while he was there, and she'd told her mother, Margaret, about him. Margaret was a devout Christian who wholeheartedly believed in the power of God, the power of prayer, and in helping those in need. Cliff believed in those things too, and with Debra and me in Florida, and Clint behind bars, Margaret and Sarah became Cliff's lifeline. They picked him up the day he got out of prison and took him to Erin's but encouraged him to come live with them. Within a matter of weeks, he did. He had his own room in their sprawling farmhouse, and a short time later, after he'd been given the right to have primary physical placement of his children, they moved in as well. They were all part of the family, and before long, Cliff and Sarah began a relationship.

Cliff and I spoke long-distance at least once a month during the two years he lived with Sarah and her family. He was content, happy to be living a quiet life, but shared that he was struggling to make ends meet. They'd helped him get a job, but it paid minimum wage—not nearly enough to cover all his bills. Court costs were expensive, and he'd needed to pay for both his past actions and the actions needed to get full custody of his kids. He was determined though, he said, to stay straight and earn every dollar legitimately.

In the summer of 2002, after more than three years of regular communication, he went silent.

After weeks of not hearing from him, I called Sarah's home.

"He's moved out," her mother, Margaret, told me. Her matter-of-fact tone caught me off guard. Margaret and I had spoken a few times during the years Cliff had lived with her family, and she'd always been pleasant.

Moved out?

"I haven't heard from him recently," she said after I asked where he might be, "but when I do, I'll let him know you called."

As uneasy as our conversation made me feel, I trusted that she would.

"I'm sure he'll come around to see the kids," she added. That bewildered me even more.

He'd left his kids with her? What had happened? And where was he?

A few months later, he would call from an apartment he was renting to tell me his relationship with Sarah had ended, and Margaret had wanted the kids to stay with them. He knew they could provide a more stable environment than he could. They were just four and five. He couldn't work and take care of them as well.

For several months, he kept in touch with me, and then inexplicably, he went silent again. By the time of our dad's accident in December of 2003, I hadn't heard from him for several months. I'd tried calling but his phone number was out of order, so I'd let it go and assumed he'd call before long.

But on that December morning after the accident, when I needed to reach him, I called Margaret. She knew exactly where Cliff was.

CHAPTER 25
Bridging the Gaps

DECEMBER 10, 2003

"Cliff's back in jail," Margaret informed me. He'd been there since July, she said, after getting arrested for selling weed within a thousand feet of a school zone.

Words from a letter he'd written to me shortly before his release three years earlier rang in my head.

I need to break this cycle of sitting time & fucking up & sitting time & fucking up. It's a waste of my life.

My heart sank with the weight of my love for him and the agony I knew he must've felt when he knew he'd lost everything he'd worked so hard for.

No wonder he hadn't called me. No wonder he hadn't written.

Upon hearing my reason for calling, Margaret expressed her concern for our dad and told me Cliff was in Manitowoc. There was no hope of Cliff joining me at the hospital but at least I could let him know what was happening and let him know that I knew where he was. And maybe, if I could talk to him, I could tell him that I loved him regardless.

I decided to try to reach Clint before calling the jail. His number from five years earlier was still in my phone. I dialed it, doubting it was good and wondering whether or not he'd answer if he knew it was me. His years of silence sent a clear message that I'd struck a nerve when I'd told him to call me after he got his shit together. Either he didn't have it together yet, or he did, and he didn't give a damn about what I thought.

His number was out of order.

Even if I could reach him, would he care about any of this? As far as I knew, he and Cliff had only seen our dad once since they'd first reunited after Cliff had turned eighteen. Clint was no longer the young boy he'd been back then. He was twenty-four now. Would this matter to him? Would he want to see our dad?

Would he be willing to see *me*?

His face flashed in my head. His blue eyes. His blonde hair. I imagined he still looked like our dad. I'd seen the resemblance when I'd met him as a teen.

Suddenly, the boys' grandmother Rose came to mind. I hadn't thought of calling her when I hadn't heard from Cliff since I'd assumed he would contact me again, but I bet she knew where both of them were.

It'd been ten years since my last call to her, back in 1993, when she'd helped me reconnect with them. I'd never told her how it went. Had they? Did she know I'd been in touch with Cliff since then? Did she know Clint and I had written for a few years but now hadn't spoken for five?

I headed toward our attic stairs planning to search for my old, pink address book when it hit me that I could now just use the Internet. I typed her name in the search bar of whitepages.com and crossed my fingers. Sure enough, her address and phone number came right up. She still lived at the farmhouse where Debra had taken me when I was a young girl. I dialed Rose's number, hoping she could again bridge a gap.

Her familiar voice answered the phone.

"I'm so sorry about your father," she said after I told her about our dad's accident. It felt as if no time had passed. I asked for Clint's number, and without hesitation, she gave it to me. If she knew that we'd broken ties, I couldn't tell.

"He's living in Manitowoc," she told me.

In Manitowoc. Where Cliff is.

"You should be able to reach him but getting a hold of Cliff might be difficult."

I knew about that, I told her, but we didn't go into details. I thanked her, hung up, and dialed Clint's number before I lost my nerve. Breaking through the barrier I'd created with him wouldn't be easy. I pushed forward without overthinking what I'd say.

"Hello?" He answered on the first ring, his midwestern accent thick, his voice deeper than I'd remembered. The last time I'd seen him, seven years earlier, he'd been a senior in high school.

I gave him a quick hello, ignored my desire to clear up our unresolved conflict, and launched into my reason for calling.

"Roy's been in an accident," I said, sensitive to the fact that he and Cliff only ever called him Roy. "A car accident. He's in critical condition at Froedtert in Milwaukee."

Not giving Clint a moment to respond, I went into the details the nurses had given me—Roy's fractured skull, the bleeding in his brain, his fractured spine, and paralysis on one side. "He's on a ventilator and has a twenty to thirty percent chance of survival." I paused for just a second to catch my breath. "I'm flying to Milwaukee tomorrow. Do you want to meet me there?"

Whew! I'd done it.

I shut up and heard him exhale into the phone. Manitowoc was less than two hours from Milwaukee.

Do you have a car to get there? I wanted to ask. *Do you have a job you need to ask off from?*

I hoped the answer to both was yes, but even if there were no obstacles, would he care enough to come?

I stayed quiet and waited for his response.

"Yeah, I do," he finally said.

My hand went to my heart.

Really?

"What about Cliff?" he asked.

Scared of saying anything that would derail our conversation, I carefully crafted my response.

"Do you think he'll be able to come?"

Another exhale came through the phone. "I'll call and see if they'll release him for the day."

My mind spun. *He might be able to come?* I hadn't expected that.

Then, knowing Clint's record was only slightly better than Cliff's, I asked if maybe I should make the call.

Clint was silent for a second, and I wondered if I'd overstepped my bounds.

"I think it'll be okay," he said flatly. "They'll call Froedtert to verify anyway."

"Okay." I said, feeling like I'd been put in my place. "I'll get in around noon tomorrow. I'll meet you at the hospital."

I clicked to hang up and the phone rang in my hand, showing my mother's number on the Caller ID. A feeling of relief flooded through me.

She and Charlie were driving through Georgia, she said, and their cell-phone service had just reconnected.

"I'm so sorry," she said before I'd even said a word. She'd

listened to a voicemail from my Aunt Dorothy. "She heard about the accident on her police scanner last night."

Knowing Dorothy's contempt for my dad, it didn't seem right that she'd been the one to tell my mom the news. Dorothy had long ago lost any affection she'd had for my dad. Having married his brother when they were all in their twenties, she'd witnessed my dad's decline for decades. My guess was she couldn't have cared less about him being in an accident. She'd likely expected it, just like I'd expected someone to call to tell me he had died.

"Is he okay?" my mom asked. I could hear the concern in her voice.

I grabbed my snowman stationery pad and read off the list of my dad's injuries that I'd just shared with Clint.

"Oh, Gina. Are you okay?"

I sat down at our kitchen table and tried to explain my mix of emotions. Over the years, I'd shared with her most of the ups and downs of my relationship with my dad. She understood my concern for him and my fear of what might come next—his death or his possible recovery.

"I'm next of kin," I told her.

"Oh, my God," I could tell it hit her like it'd hit me. "I guess you are."

"And I'm flying to Milwaukee in the morning," I said matter-of-factly.

"You are?" She was surprised. I thought she might be.

"My flight leaves at eight."

She was silent for a moment.

"I was thinking about him last night," she said finally. "We stopped to get dinner at Subway, and while we were waiting in line, a song came on in the restaurant that always reminds me of him."

I imagined my dad the night before, lying on the ground at the corner of Eighth Street and Center Avenue in Sheboygan, barely alive, but telepathically dialing up Casey Kasem and asking for a long-distance dedication.

Casey, would you please play "Everything I Own" by Bread. For Sharon. She'll know who it's from.

It was a song I knew by heart, and I knew why it spoke to her.

After she'd ended their seven-year marriage, my dad—like the lyrics expressed—would have given anything to have her back again. She'd loved him, and though she'd gone back and forth, more for his sake and mine than for her own, she ultimately decided she wasn't willing to live the unstable life that he was comfortable with. She'd wanted to know the bills would get paid and her husband would come straight home from work instead of stopping at a corner bar. She'd wanted more than he could give, and even though he'd been willing to give everything, it hadn't been enough.

"Is anyone else going with you?" my mom asked now, circling back to my impending trip.

"Tara was working when I called this morning," I told her. "Sherry said she'd call me back, but I don't know if she'll come. But Peggy is." Peggy, my best friend since childhood, still lived near Milwaukee. I'd called her before calling Margaret, to tell her the news and to see if she could be with me. At the time, I'd expected she might be the only one. "She's coming after she gets off work and staying at the hotel with me. And Clint is coming, too. Maybe even Cliff." I filled her in on Cliff's situation.

"I hope they can all make it," she said. "Wouldn't that be something."

She and Charlie would come to our house that Saturday, she said, on their way home from vacation. I'd already be back from Wisconsin by then, and I was grateful I'd get to hug her at the end of it all.

"It's good that you're going," she said before we hung up.

"And Gina, when you see him, hold his hand and tell him I used to love him."

I told her I would and hung up, wishing instead that I could've crawled through the phone line to hug her right then.

From my seat at the kitchen table, I eyed the suitcase sitting outside my bedroom door. I'd spent so much time on the phone that morning, I hadn't even started to pack.

Instead of getting up, I called Froedtert one more time.

Nothing had changed, the nurse informed me. He was still unresponsive. Sedated.

I'd expected as much. I let her know at least one brother was coming. Maybe two. We hung up, and I grabbed my suitcase and rolled it into my room.

Clint called minutes later to tell me Cliff would get a twelve-hour pass. Clint would pick him up in the morning, and they'd meet me at the hospital. It was a lot to imagine happening, and I was both grateful they were coming and nervous about seeing them. It'd been so long, and this was not the way I'd have chosen for it to happen. Regardless, three of my dad's children were now set to be at his bedside. It was more than I'd thought possible.

Then Tara called.

"Hey." Her voice was barely above a whisper.

We hadn't seen each other since our week at the beach two years earlier, but I could picture her clear as day, holding the receiver against her sweet face, twisting the cord through her long fingers. Her wisps of white-blond hair falling in front of her eyes.

"Hi," I said, feeling apprehensive about this delicate situation. I hoped she would meet me at the hospital, but more so, for her own sake, I hoped she'd take this opportunity to see our dad, as it might be her only chance.

"You talked with your mom?" I asked.

"Yeah." She paused. "Wow . . ." She spoke in an out-of-body

sort of way, interested but disconnected at the same time. I couldn't read her.

"She told you I'm going to Milwaukee tomorrow?"

"Yeah."

She was giving me nothing.

"Do you want to meet me at the hospital?" I held my breath and waited, hoping against hope. Maybe she'd come if only to see me. She lived just an hour away.

It suddenly occurred to me that if she said yes, the four of us—me, Cliff, Clint, and Tara—would be together for the first time ever. I was thirty-five and had two children of my own, yet I'd never been in the same room with Cliff, Clint, and Tara. She'd never even met our brothers, though they all lived just thirty minutes apart. Perhaps, finally, we'd all be together.

"I have to work," Tara said, her voice soft and low. I remembered her mentioning something about a tanning salon in a recent letter to me.

"Oh." I was crushed. Devastated. Even though the thought of us all being together had only just then come to mind, it hurt to let the dream die. What could I say to make her realize the importance of being there? Maybe she didn't want to go but didn't know how to tell me. Maybe she didn't have to work. I chided myself the second I thought that. Everything had happened so quickly. She likely did have to work.

"I'll see if I can get off though," she added. It came out as more of a question than a declaration, making me wonder if she sensed my disappointment and was just placating me. Or maybe she felt obliged—to see me or to meet him.

"Really?" I was thrilled and willing to accept any reason she had as long as it meant she would come. "That would be great. I'd love to see you."

I gave her my flight times.

"Cliff and Clint are coming, too," I added, thinking maybe

I should've told her that to begin with, but then again, maybe this was all too much.

"I'd like to meet them," she said, surprising me with her enthusiasm.

My whole being filled with joy. Was it possible that everything would work out and we'd all be together?

Tara called back that evening to tell me she got her shift covered. As soon as the words were out of her mouth, I pictured the four of us in one room—we were like puzzle pieces that were finally going to get put together.

Everything felt so right.

Gone was my concern about reuniting with Cliff and Clint. My heart raced with anticipation.

"But my boyfriend can't get off work," she added, "and we need to take his car."

What?

I didn't know who this boyfriend was or why—when it looked as if the planets were finally aligning—everything should suddenly depend on a person who wasn't even part of the equation.

His schedule? *His* car? Why didn't she have a car of her own? Why were things not working out the way I wanted them to?

"We're both off on Friday though," she offered. "Can we maybe meet you in the morning? What time does your plane leave?"

After getting a glimpse of what could've been, I wasn't happy with anything less.

"My flight leaves at twenty after two," I told her, hardly disguising my disappointment. "But I have to be at the airport around noon. And Cliff and Clint can only be there on Thursday."

They wouldn't get to meet. We wouldn't all get to be together. I hoped she'd be moved by the urgency.

"I wish I could be there with all of you," she said.

Not badly enough. The words sprang to my head. I was being unfair to her, I knew, but we were so close to being together, it frustrated me that she wasn't trying harder.

Maybe there was no urgency for her. Being that the three of them lived so close to each other, maybe after this, they would meet up on their own. When Cliff got out of jail, they could figure something out.

But I wouldn't be there. After years of knowing the three of them individually, I felt I'd earned the right to be there when they met. Selfish though it was, I didn't want it to happen in my absence.

"I know you do," I said, trying to accept the situation. Maybe she really did want to be there with all of us. Maybe I was selling her short, and she was frustrated that she couldn't be. "Maybe another time," I said. "I'll call you tomorrow from the hospital after we talk with the doctors."

At least she was coming on Friday. I'd see her. She'd see our dad.

And though that was monumental on its own, I longed for more.

CHAPTER 26
Making Room

DECEMBER 11, 2003

My plane took off from Tallahassee shortly after eight in the morning. I settled into my economy seat and tried to imagine the day ahead. After a quick layover, I'd land in Milwaukee around noon. I'd take a taxi to the hospital where Cliff and Clint would be waiting for me. I assumed we'd see our dad shortly after that. But that's where my vision ended. What would happen next?

Just what would the doctors say? And what exactly did the hospital staff want from me?

Each conversation I'd had with a nurse had left me feeling as though they weren't giving me the whole story. Why did I have to be there in person to learn all the details?

My stomach tightened.

By showing up, would I suddenly become responsible for him? Financially or otherwise? Would I be expected to take him home if he survived? Or pay for arrangements if he didn't?

The airplane's seatbelt sign dinged, and a flight attendant came on the loudspeaker to tell us we were now at cruising altitude. We could move freely around the cabin. I couldn't move at all. What was I heading into?

I glanced at the carry-on bag I'd stowed beneath the seat in front of me. A spiral notebook and ballpoint pen were in there. I'd packed them to take notes at the hospital, but it seemed now I needed them for a much larger purpose.

During my life, I'd written more than a hundred poems, almost always when I was hurting. Pouring out my thoughts and feelings on pages of pretty white paper had always soothed me.

Though I'd written countless poems—after breakups, when leaving Wisconsin to move to Florida, after losing Grandma Wilsing—I'd never written one about my dad. I'd never written anything about my dad. None of our history together. None of my feelings, except for two letters I'd written to him. The one when I was sixteen, after I'd learned Sherry and Tara were gone, and another one that my therapist suggested I write when I was in my mid-twenties. Not to send to him, she'd said, but to see what I had to say. To dive deeper into what I felt at that time and to explore how I'd felt in the past. I'd scribbled more than ten pages. It had been liberating.

It seemed odd to me now, as I headed to see him for the first time in seven years, that of all the relationships in my life, I'd never written about ours.

Before landing in Milwaukee, I suddenly knew I needed to write everything. And a poem wasn't going to cut it. I needed to pour out my heart and my hurt and every thought in my head until our history was outside of my body. I needed to empty my mind of all that had come before to make room for what would come next.

I lifted the heavy shade of the little window by my side, and for a few minutes, watched the clouds roll by. The beverage cart came down the aisle, and a cold drink was offered. I declined. I reached for my notebook and pen and turned down my table tray.

Finally, this day has come, I began.

I wrote until we landed for our layover in Charlotte.

Roy is my dad, but I haven't called him that in a very long time.

And continued writing as we flew toward Milwaukee.

Our separation came following his third divorce.

I wrote about Debra, Cliff, Clint, Sherry, Tara, and Grandma. I wrote about our cancelled Christmas and the letter my mother had shared with him. I wrote about the weekend retreat and reconnecting and about the last time I'd seen him and about the call I'd received just two days earlier telling me he'd been in an accident. I wrote how I was feeling right then.

I have often thought about writing him a letter to tell him the good things I remember. Now I will tell him in person and hope that somewhere beneath the tubes and the ventilator he will hear me and he will know I am there.

The pilot's voice came over the loudspeaker and announced we'd be landing soon. It was just before noon. I took off my glasses and sopped up my tears with the sleeve of my sweater. I'd let them fall freely as I was writing, not wanting to interrupt my thoughts to wipe them away. It had hurt to remember. And it had been healing as well.

I found the granola bar I'd packed in my carry-on, tore open the package, and took a bite. Then double checked my wallet to be sure I had the cash I thought I'd brought. I did. I expected Cliff and Clint had already arrived at Froedtert. And I went back to writing.

Suddenly I'm nervous. I'll land in Milwaukee and get to the hospital and Cliff and Clint will be there. I'll check in at the Family Care Center and they'll take us to him. And I'll see him. I'm so nervous and I don't know why exactly. The emotional overload, I imagine.

I can't believe this is really happening. I keep thinking it's a dream.

A long thought in my head about what might happen in the future. That's exactly what it feels like.

This is really happening and it is mind-boggling.

I looked up from my notebook. I'd done it—emptied myself of every thought and feeling that stuck out in my memory, put all the details I'd carried around for so many years on the pages in front of me. Eighteen pages. I felt purged. Released. Like an empty vessel. At least as I headed into the rest of the day, I had that.

The plane touched down just before noon, and the pilot welcomed us to Milwaukee.

"Where the temperature is twenty-four degrees," he added.

Welcome back to Wisconsin.

The taxi ride to the hospital took just twenty minutes. There was no winter-white snow falling from the sky like I'd hoped there might be. There wasn't even any snow on the ground. Everything was just gray.

I stepped out of the taxi, got my suitcase from the driver, and stared up at the mammoth, multi-storied building. The wall of windows turned my thoughts to all the rooms inside. And all the people in all those rooms. My dad was one of them. Soon, I would be too.

CHAPTER 27
Ready or Not

Froedtert's lobby was huge and ultra-bright white—like I imagine the lobby of Heaven might look. And just like I imagine Heaven's lobby might feel, it was both comforting and overwhelming. The ceiling seemed to reach to the sky, and there were more chairs than I could count. A quick sweep of the room told me Cliff and Clint weren't there yet. It hadn't occurred to me that I might beat them to the hospital.

Now what?

The reception desk was across the room. All I had to do was walk over and check in, and I'd be whisked to my dad's room in no time.

So, go, I told myself. But my feet wouldn't move. My hand gripped the handle of my suitcase. I stared wide-eyed at everyone in the place.

I should wait, I told myself. For Cliff and Clint. Of course. I mean, how could I go up without them? They were expecting to meet me in the lobby. I had to be here for them.

And yet, the moment was here. I'd convinced myself to

come, and I'd driven and flown and taxied and written my way here. I'd done everything I could to prepare.

And yet.

I still wasn't ready.

I wasn't ready to move forward. To face him. To see him. To talk to him. To be with him.

I just wasn't ready.

Pulling my suitcase behind me, I walked in the opposite direction of the reception area. If someone noticed me, they'd ask me to check in. I couldn't take that risk.

I had just sat down, stacking my carry-on bag and purse on my lap to build a shield of sorts, when my phone buzzed in my purse. Rattled by the noise, I scrambled to dig it out and flipped it open. I hoped it was Cliff or Clint calling to say they were in the parking lot and would be right in. Instead, I found Tara on the line.

"We're coming today!" I could hear the brightness in her voice.

"What?" It didn't quite sink in.

"Jake's getting off work early, and we're coming today! Okay? It'll be late—around four o'clock—but we'll be there."

I glanced at my watch. In just a few hours, Cliff, Clint, Tara, and I would be together for the first time in our lives.

"That's so great!" I told her. "I got here a little while ago, and Cliff and Clint should be here any minute."

"Have you seen him already?" she asked, referring to Roy, but not saying his name.

An image came to mind of our dad lying in his sterile hospital bed in one of the rooms on one of the floors above me. *I should be there already.*

"No," I said, "I'm waiting for Cliff and Clint. We'll wait for you before we make any decisions—if there are any to be made."

"You don't have to wait for me. I'm just glad I can be with all of you tonight. I'll call you when we're on our way."

We hung up, and I closed my phone. It hit me that we—Roy's four children—would be filing into the hospital in our birth order. I was here, the boys would arrive next, and Tara would come last.

We're all going to be together. It ran through my mind over and over. We'd be together and we'd be with him.

Cliff and Clint and Tara would meet, and I'd be right there with them.

Tara would see her father for the first time since she was two, and we'd get to help her through it.

How miraculous and strange it all seemed.

The hospital clock read a quarter past one. *Where are my brothers?* My fingers tapped repeatedly on my purse. My feet wiggled back and forth. I had to tell someone I was here. Now. The hours I had, on this day and this day only, were slipping away. I had to do whatever needed to be done.

I gathered my belongings and headed to check in.

"You can have a seat," the lady said, not realizing I'd already been sitting. "They'll call you up soon."

I took my bags back to my spot and was about to sit when my phone buzzed again. This time, it was Clint.

"We're close," he said.

Close? You're not here?

"About thirty minutes away."

Lord, what was taking so long?

"Have you seen him yet?"

"No," I told him. Despite my concern about time, it was so good to hear his voice. "I just checked in. I'm waiting to go up." I let him know I'd have to turn off my phone before entering the ICU. "When you come, just check in, and I think they'll bring you to the room. Oh, and Tara called! She's coming tonight with her boyfriend."

"Really?" The excitement in his voice matched what I'd heard in Tara's. "I can't wait to meet her."

My heart swelled.

We were moving forward, ready or not. Surely, I could handle whatever came next, even if I had to face it alone at first. Cliff and Clint would be here soon. Tara would be here later. Maybe all that really mattered was that we would be together. Come what may.

I flipped my phone closed and tucked it into the side pocket of my carry-on. I'd heard from everyone except Peggy, but I knew she'd be on her way when her workday ended.

The receptionist called out my maiden name, and I stood up. Even though I wasn't that girl anymore, and I didn't go by that name, I realized—after writing for hours on the plane and working through my anxiety in the lobby—that she was a part of me forever. As was my dad. As were my siblings.

"Right here." I raised my hand, feeling very much like that young girl I'd once been. Back when my dad's silly jokes had been the funniest thing in the world to me and his hugs had made me feel loved.

Back when I'd been his Bessers.

I handed my suitcase to the receptionist who offered to store it for me and turned my attention to the nurse who'd lead me to my father's room. I fixed my eyes on the heels of her silent white shoes as we entered the elevator, grateful to focus on something simple as we made our journey to him. Trying not to overthink or over-feel in the moment.

We arrived on the third floor and walked past a large sign with red letters notifying me that I was entering the Neurological Intensive Care Unit. My mind separated from my body a bit as I took it all in. The stark white walls. The long, empty hallways. The silver railings decorated with strings of green garland.

Oh, yes, Christmas.

"Please have a seat," the nurse said.

I looked at her, confused.

"Someone will be with you shortly."

She motioned for me to sit in the small ICU waiting room. Then she walked away on her silent white shoes and left me alone again with my thoughts. I hadn't expected another moment to catch my breath, but I was grateful for it. Maybe the hospital had been designed with this little space in mind, not just because we needed an area in which to wait, but because people might need just another minute to gather their thoughts. I looked out the only window in the room, focusing on the tiny beams of light sneaking out from behind the gray clouds.

It was possible my brothers would get here before the nurse came back—they were probably twenty minutes away—but it was looking more likely that I'd go in alone.

Maybe that's how it was meant to be. Just me and my dad. No buffer.

I'd see him.

Oh, my God, I'd *see* him!

I'd spent so much time and energy fretting over the emotional part of being in the same room with him that I hadn't really thought about how he would look. He'd crashed his bicycle into a car. His head had hit the windshield. He hadn't been wearing a helmet. Would there be lacerations? Bumps? Bruises? Blood?

And would he even know I was there? When I spoke to him, even though he was unresponsive, would he be able to hear me? I'd read that comatose people could hear, but now I wondered if that was just something we told ourselves in order to feel better.

Even if he could hear me, though, would he recognize the sound of my voice? I was thirty-five and had hardly spoken to him in twenty years. How would he know it was me?

How I wished I could've found the cassette tape I'd wanted to bring with me. On it, I'd recorded myself singing all my favorite songs on Thanksgiving Day 1975, when I was just seven years old.

My dad had given me one of those bulky cassette-tape recorders with the big fat buttons, and he and Grandma had been my audience while I sang songs I'd learned in Brownies and in school, and songs I knew from listening to my dad.

And some songs, I just made up on the spot. One about how much I loved my mom and dad, and one about the back brace he'd been wearing for two months, ever since he'd run his car off the road on an overpass. He'd shot through the guardrail and landed in the treetops below, breaking several ribs.

"When I get to take this thing off," he'd told me, "I'm gonna hang it from the antenna on the top of the Security First National Bank downtown."

It cracked me up to imagine his big old brace hanging from the antenna of that seven-story building, the highest one in town. How funny it would be for everyone to see it banging around in the wind. I thought he might actually do it.

Of course, I didn't know the truth behind the accident back then. That he'd been arrested for drunk driving and a hit-and-run that had caused property damage even before he'd hit the guardrail. I didn't know he'd pleaded no contest, had paid a hefty fine, and had to take a driving course so he could keep his license. He'd been just thirty-one at the time. I didn't know he was lucky to be alive.

Before I'd left Tallahassee, I'd scoured my box of old cassette tapes hoping to find that one. I'd wanted to bring my Walkman and put my headphones on his ears and play it for him. I'd felt sure he would recognize that voice. Besser's voice. And that even if he couldn't open his eyes or speak, he would give me a sign to let me know he knew I was there. Maybe he still would, but it seemed less likely now that I had only my adult voice to rely on.

A nurse appeared in the doorway of the waiting room.

"You can see him now."

I looked up at her, my wide eyes staring into her sympathetic ones. I threw my carry-on bag and purse over my shoulder and checked the time on my watch. It was almost one-thirty.

Are my brothers here yet?

I didn't ask, and she didn't say.

I took a quick look out the window as I passed by it, as if I'd be able to see their car or catch a glimpse of them walking up. *When would they get here?*

The nurse turned back to be sure I was following her, and I realized it didn't matter anymore.

I was going in alone. My time was up.

CHAPTER 28
All I Wanted

My eyes fell again to the nurse's shoes as she led me down a long, white hallway and past a nurses' station. I could barely feel my feet as I followed her. I was there but not there. Watching myself make my way to my dad.

She stopped at a door, and I stopped behind her. I guessed we were right outside of his room. I took a deep breath, heard the latch click, and watched as the door slowly swung open. Head down, I followed the nurse a few feet into the room.

"Let us know if you need anything," she said, and then she left.

The heaviness of the moment hit me, and I closed my eyes. Not only had I finally arrived in his room, but for the first time in nearly twenty years I was alone with him. Since the day he'd driven me home after giving me birthday presents and belated Christmas gifts and telling me Sherry and Tara were gone. How sad to think I'd seen him only twice in all that time— once with Grandma and once with Larry.

I thought back to the message I'd written on my Aunt Eunice's Christmas letter the previous December. The note I'd asked her to share with him: *Tell him I said hello. Life is too short.* Now, in mere seconds, I'd tell him hello myself and within the hour, perhaps I'd find out just how short his life might be.

The gentle whirring of the machines in the room pulled me from my thoughts, and I knew it was time to move forward. Glancing down, I watched my feet shuffle toward the bed, until finally within a foot of it, I looked up at him.

My breath caught in my throat.

There he was. In the flesh. Tucked in on three sides, eyes closed, immobile. But there was a beauty about him. Other than a few scratches on his forehead, there were no signs of trauma. His dark blond hair was parted to one side, just like he always styled it. His face looked fresh and clean. He appeared younger than he had the last time I'd seen him seven years before. Healthier. Even handsome. Like the dad I remembered from my childhood.

I cocked my head, feeling the pang of missing that dad.

My eyes moved to the I.V. tube plugged into a vein on his right hand. I wanted to touch his fingers but couldn't make myself do it. I told myself I was afraid of disturbing him, but at my core, I wasn't ready to make a physical connection. I still needed time to adjust.

Instead, I wrapped my fingers around the silver guardrail of his bed and started talking.

"Hi," I began softly. I scanned his face for a reaction, ready to call for a nurse if he moved the slightest bit.

He didn't.

I leaned in closer.

"I'm here," I said, a bit louder.

The blanket that covered his chest rose and fell in time with the rhythmic whirs, but he didn't stir.

"It's me, Dad," I said. "It's Bessers. I'm here."

Still no reaction. I was here. I'd come back. How could he not respond? Of course, I knew it was beyond his choosing.

He had a long list of injuries. I just couldn't see them. He had bleeding in his brain, and every nurse I'd talked to had told me that he was unresponsive. But I'd still held out hope that he'd be responsive to me.

To *me*.

But he wasn't. He gave me nothing.

I scanned his body from head to toe. Discouraged. Disheartened.

Maybe he'll wake up while we're here. Maybe. Then again, was that what I was hoping for?

It was one thing to have him lie still with his eyes closed and give me a sign that he knew I was there. It would be quite another if he were fully conscious, able to open his eyes, able to have a conversation.

Back home when I first got the call, I would've been fine had he regained consciousness. I'd hoped for it. It would've meant he was okay, and I wouldn't have had to come up and be his next of kin. But I was here, and that changed everything.

Now if he woke up, we'd have to talk—about the past seven years and why he hadn't written and where we'd go from here. Had not acknowledging him as my father in my engagement announcement been a rejection he couldn't understand? Maybe he'd thought I just didn't care. Maybe he'd thought I didn't need him.

If he woke up now, how could I leave? When he got released from the hospital, where would he go? Not The Salvation Army. Who did he have other than me? He wasn't going to live with Aunt Eunice.

Maybe he'd wake up for just a little while. Just long enough for us to say we loved each other. And then we'd get a proper goodbye.

Just give me a sign! I wanted to shout.

Maybe it was too late. Maybe he was already gone.

I stared at his face, expecting to cry at the thought of that.

Not because I would miss him in my daily life but because I would miss the opportunity to ever have him in my life again.

The tears didn't come.

Instead, a sense of relief washed over me. If he died, I'd be forever released from the responsibility of trying to figure out this relationship. We'd be done. I'd be free.

Was it terrible of me to feel that it would be easier to lose my dad forever than to have him survive and still choose not to have me in his life?

I was back to just wanting a sign. I didn't want him to wake up. I didn't want to have a conversation.

The little girl in me longed for a hug. The teen in me still struggled with being angry. The young woman in me had grown to forgive him. And as I stood at his bedside, now, all I wanted was for him to know I was there.

Had he been able to utter just one sentence, I would've wanted it to be, *Aww, Bessers—you're here.*

A soft knock at the door interrupted my thoughts.

"Excuse me—Miss Wilsing?" It was the nurse who had brought me to the room.

I straightened up and let go of the guardrail. It seemed only a few minutes had gone by.

She opened the door just slightly and poked her head in.

"I'm sorry to disturb you," she said softly, "but your brothers are here."

I held my breath and waited for them to walk through the door.

CHAPTER 29
The Only Card I Had

Cliff and Clint strode in, their heads up, their eyes searching the room. These boys, my brothers, were now men. Cliff led the way, heading straight to the bedrail where I'd stood just a minute before. Clint followed behind. They each gave me a nod hello—not a hug or a *How are you?*—and then turned their focus to our dad.

I hadn't yet uttered a word when Cliff abruptly turned away, shook his head, and started back toward the door.

"Is there a place to have a smoke around here?" he asked the nurse.

A smoke? He'd just gotten here. Was he serious?

The nurse looked from him to me. Cliff raised his eyebrows and waited for her reply.

"Of course," she said. I imagined she'd seen this response before. "Take the elevator back down to the first floor. There's an open courtyard right off the main lobby."

Cliff nodded and walked out with Clint at his heels.

I understood Cliff's reaction, but I wasn't taking it as well as the nurse. Now that I was finally here, I didn't want to leave my dad, but if I wanted to talk with my brothers, I'd have to.

This was no longer about just my own needs. I had them to take care of.

I didn't know how many times they'd seen our dad since they'd reunited with him as teens, and they didn't have as many memories of him as I had, but they obviously had a bond. They'd come because he mattered to them.

I glanced at the nurse who was now checking the monitors. "Is it okay if I go with them?"

"Yes, of course," she said. "Just have someone buzz me when you're back."

I looked longingly at our dad and followed the nurse into the hallway where I found Cliff and Clint waiting by the elevator.

"The doctors will be available to meet with you shortly," she said and went on her way.

We stepped into the elevator, and Cliff hit the button for the lobby. Neither of them said a word—about what the doctors might say or how our dad had looked or how they were feeling. And I didn't know how to begin the conversation.

The doors opened and we spotted a vending machine close by.

"How 'bout a soda?" Clint asked.

He bought me a Diet Coke and got a Sprite for himself. Cliff wrinkled his nose at the offer. He was more interested in going out for a smoke. Clint and I popped open our sodas and followed him to the courtyard. The cold can in my hand felt even colder when the wind hit me. With only a sweater on, the chill ran through me. We were alone in the wide-open cemented space, and the sky above was oppressively gray.

Cliff wasn't bothered by the weather. He dug into the pockets of his jeans and pulled out a pack of cigarettes and a lighter. Clint took a sip of his soda, and I followed suit just to give myself something to do.

Then the big sister in me kicked in. It was the only card I had, and I had to play it.

"You know," I began, "You can tell me anything."

Neither of them met my gaze. Cliff lit his cigarette, and Clint took another sip of soda.

"I mean," I continued, pushing my words out into what felt like a wall of resistance, "whatever you're feeling—angry, sad, indifferent—it's okay to feel it. We can talk about it." I sipped on my soda and waited.

Cliff fixed his gaze on the ground and blew a stream of smoke into the wind. "When they told me my dad was in the hospital," he said, "I wondered which one it was."

Clint looked up at him and then looked away.

"When did you last see him?" I asked gently.

"About a year ago," Clint said. He set his soda on the brick ledge next to him and dug his hands into the pockets of his jeans. "We played pool with him at The Salvation Army in Appleton."

"Why were you there?" I looked at Cliff, hoping he'd add to the conversation, but he just looked at Clint.

"That's where he was living," Clint said. "We met him there one night."

Our dad had been living at The Salvation Army? All those years I hadn't heard from him, I'd pictured him living with a friend or in some tiny apartment. I'd never imagined he was at a shelter.

"I didn't know," I confessed, feeling my world had flipped upside down. They knew more about our dad than I did. "Why was he in Appleton?" It was more than an hour from Sheboygan.

"I guess you can only stay in a shelter for so long before they make you move on," Clint said. "His time at the Sheboygan one was up." He shrugged. "Anyway, that was the last time we saw him." He took his hands from his pockets and rubbed them together.

I wanted to know more but my feet were freezing, and I couldn't take another sip of cold soda. Cliff seemed to read my mind. He maneuvered around me to crush his cigarette in an ashtray sitting on a nearby ledge. His blue-gray eyes met mine for just a moment.

"We should probably get back up there, eh?"

"Yeah," I said, surrendering my desire to reach out and hug him. "We probably should."

We returned to the lobby where I let the receptionist know we were ready, and we were whisked back to the ICU waiting room. I looked out the only window in the room.

Clint took a seat, closed his eyes, and leaned his head back against the wall. To my surprise, Cliff came to my side and for a few seconds, we stood together gazing out at the gray clouds.

Feeling brave, I put my arm around his shoulders.

Within seconds, his body relaxed, and he laid his head to rest on me. The tears that hadn't come to me at our dad's bedside welled up now.

"I love you," I whispered, still staring out into the sky.

"I love you too," Cliff whispered back, and he turned to give me the hug I'd been hoping for.

"Miss Wilsing?" The nurse was back all too soon.

Cliff and I turned to face her, and Clint sat up in his chair.

"I'll be taking you to a counseling room now where the doctors will meet with you."

Clint rose to join us. Cliff took my hand. And together, the three of us followed the nurse to learn the fate of our father.

Part Five

CHAPTER 30
No More Swiveling

We were the first ones to arrive in the dimly lit conference room on the fifth floor.

"Please have a seat." The nurse motioned for us to sit in the red leather swivel chairs placed around a large table in the middle of the small room. We sat next to each other on one end. She sat on a nearby couch, leaving the remaining chairs for the doctors and other staff she said would be joining us soon.

This is life or death. The three of us said nothing but it had to be what we were all thinking.

Will he live or will he die? We would soon find out.

After wrestling with my thoughts at his bedside, I'd leaned toward the oddly comfortable thought of him dying because of the relief it would bring, but now the idea of his death brought up new questions and fears. I needed to find out if being next of kin meant I'd be responsible for him. My thoughts turned from the emotional side of things to the financial.

If he died, would I be responsible for the hospital bill? His funeral? His burial?

Who else would be?

And how much would all of that cost?

Would I be expected to arrange those things? From Florida?

And even if I did, who would I be doing it for? Other than the three of us, and maybe Tara and my Aunt Eunice, who would possibly come to his funeral?

I thought of my mother and her preference to be cremated. Would that be a less expensive option?

I swiveled in my chair, feeling restless and running on nervous energy. Cliff and Clint swiveled too.

The door opened and suddenly the room filled with people in white coats until there was barely enough room to move. Barely enough air to breathe.

They introduced themselves. A few were doctors. A couple were nurses. One was a social worker.

One of the doctors began telling us about the damage to our dad's frontal lobe. A nurse added that his head had been full of blood. As they went on, their voices began to merge and sound far away, as if they were at one end of a tunnel and I were on the other side.

They gave details about the accident. He'd been riding his bicycle, they said. Without a helmet. In the dark. In the business district where bicycles aren't allowed.

He'd run into a moving vehicle. It had not hit him.

His head had smashed into the windshield, leaving a spider web of cracks in the glass. He'd landed on the pavement, they told us, face down.

I pictured him lying there. My vision blurred, and I wrapped my arms around myself.

The boys sat frozen in their chairs.

Someone at the Sheboygan hospital, they said, had contacted my Aunt Eunice. She'd told them our dad's last place of residence had been The Salvation Army in Sheboygan.

According to their records, he'd been living there or at the one in Appleton for more than two years.

My dad had been homeless for *two years*, and I hadn't known.

I should've known.

Someone should've told me, or I should've felt something internally—the way twins can sense when something is wrong with their sibling. Maybe I could've done something for him. Maybe I could've helped somehow.

A nurse said she'd spoken with a woman at the shelter who'd said our dad had been working there as a temp, doing odd jobs to earn a bit of money. She wasn't aware of any of his medical conditions other than alcoholism, and he hadn't been interested in treatment for that.

His time at the Sheboygan shelter had been up that Monday, she said. He'd left, and she didn't know where he'd gone. She was sad to hear about his accident Tuesday night.

The three of us sat listening, trying to take it all in.

The doctors switched gears, telling us about his condition the night he arrived.

His level of consciousness, determined by a system of evaluation called the Glasgow Coma Scale, was severely low. He hadn't responded to voice commands or withdrawn from pain. He'd uttered unintelligible sounds, and he hadn't opened his eyes. On the scale from three to fifteen, three being the most severely unconscious, he'd scored a six.

He'd been intubated to protect his airway, they said. The machine was doing his breathing for him.

I could hear the whirring in my head.

CT scans showed five fractures on his skull, mostly on the left and back sides.

He had multiple fractured ribs, and his lungs were inflamed.

Several discs in his cervical spine—between the base of his

skull and his upper torso—had been damaged, and he'd lost some spinal function. His right extremities moved spontaneously. His left extremities hadn't moved at all.

I shifted in my seat and looked at my brothers. Their faces were long. Their eyes wide open. Cliff was likely hearing most of this for the first time, and I imagined Clint hadn't remembered everything I'd read off to him from my scribbled notes on the snowman stationery. I hardly remembered it all.

Our dad had had an operation to establish ventricular drainage, they said. Ten tubes had been placed to drain fluid from the ventricles of his brain. To keep them decompressed and to monitor intracranial pressure. A ventricular shunt had been inserted to relieve pressure inside the skull due to the excess fluid.

His temperature had risen to 103.3, for which he'd been given Tylenol.

And he'd vomited.

They kept coming back to him being unresponsive—just like he'd been while I was in the room. But they hadn't yet mentioned whether they thought he'd live or die.

And then they did.

The lead neurologist took the floor.

"The part of the brain that's been damaged affects personality and speech," he began.

Personality. That defined my dad.

"It regulates attention, emotion, and memory," the doctor explained. "Even if he were to survive his injuries, he would have to learn to do everything all over again—eat, walk, talk."

A vision of my dad at my home in Florida flashed in my mind. What I saw wasn't the dad from my childhood or even the man I'd just seen lying so peacefully in bed a few floors below. What I saw was a man I hardly recognized. Sitting on the couch in my living room. Waiting to be spoon-fed because he couldn't feed himself. I imagined helping him walk to the bathroom because he was too weak to make it there alone. I saw a helpless man I didn't want to help.

What had happened to the compassion I'd felt when I'd learned he was homeless? Why wouldn't I want to help him recover? He was still my dad.

"Because of the extent of his injuries," the doctor's voice interrupted my thoughts, "it would be unlikely that he'd have an independent life. He'd never be able to function on his own again."

My hand shot to my mouth.

Oh, my God.

I looked at my brothers who were looking back at me—all of us speechless.

"You have two options," the doctor said. "You can have him continue on the ventilator or you can withdraw care."

I sat in stunned silence. I remembered Nurse Sally telling me over the phone that my family and I would need to think about what we'd like to do. I hadn't really thought it would come to that. I'd thought the decision would be made for us. Gathering the family had been my focus, not deciding what we'd like to do.

What we'd like to do. As if we'd be given a choice.

But now we had been.

I planted my elbows on the table in front of me and clasped my hands together.

I was next of kin, but really, who was I to make this decision? How was that a thing a person was expected to do?

He'd never be himself again, they'd said. He'd have to relearn everything, they'd said.

Were they *absolutely sure*?

If I chose to take him off life support, would I really be doing it because it was in his best interest? Or because it was in mine?

I looked again to Cliff and Clint. They'd hardly moved. No more nervous energy. No more swiveling.

"Take your time," a nurse said. "Take some time to talk."

Some of the doctors and nurses politely excused themselves. Some stayed, as did the social worker.

Cliff, Clint, and I rolled our chairs just beyond the edge of the table and turned to face each other, our knees almost touching.

His personality wouldn't be his own, we reminded each other.

His memory would be altered. His speech would be impaired.

He'd have no quality of life, we said. He'd never live independently again. The doctors had made that clear, and we all agreed our dad wouldn't want that.

I turned to face the group.

"We'll withdraw care," I said to the doctors.

Everyone in the tiny conference room solemnly nodded.

"But not right away," I was quick to add. "Our sister Tara's coming in about an hour, and we want her to be able to spend some time with him."

Of course, they said. We could take all the time we needed. We could go back to the ICU waiting room, and they would send Tara to us when she arrived. The doctors and nurses filed out of the room, and we rose to follow them. We were almost out the door when the social worker approached me.

"Would you like to request a chaplain?" she asked.

A chaplain? I was still processing the decision we'd just made, and she was already moving onto the next step. One I hadn't even thought about.

My dad and I had never spoken about religion, but I knew he'd been raised Lutheran, as had I. And even though I tended to lean away from organized religion, I believed that he believed.

"Yes," I told the social worker. "A chaplain would be nice."

We turned to a nurse, who led my brothers and me back down to the third floor to spend whatever time remained with our dad.

CHAPTER 31
What Sucks Now

We had just gotten off the elevator on the third floor when Cliff turned to the nurse.

"Could I go to his room now?" he asked her. We hadn't talked about who would go first, but I was glad he was willing. Clint gave him a nod, I gave him a hug, and we watched him walk away with the nurse.

From the age of eleven, when he'd first learned about our dad, he'd hoped to have a relationship with him, and he'd so looked forward to meeting him when he turned eighteen. But in the seven years that followed their reunion, I didn't know how often they'd kept in touch. Only once during that time had Cliff mentioned hearing from him.

Cliff wrote to me from jail in November 1999, saying he'd received a letter. It had been nearly four years since he had met our dad.

He moved to Manitowoc, Cliff had written, *because he thinks people are more friendly there.*

He said he'd like to get to know me better and get together in the future. And he'd like to teach me how to install carpeting. It's a good trade. He's done it for 33 years and likes it.

It shocked me to hear from him. I wrote back. We'll see what happens.

Nothing happened that I knew of, other than Cliff and Clint visiting him four years after that at The Salvation Army in Appleton. I didn't know what Cliff wanted to say or do during his time with our dad—maybe he didn't know either—but he was going to spend time with him, and that was a good start. I hoped he'd emerge with a sense of closure if nothing else.

I looked at my watch. It was a quarter to four, close to the time Tara said she and Jake would arrive.

"Wanna go to the cafeteria while we wait? See what they have?" Clint suggested.

I wasn't hungry, but I hadn't had anything since the granola bar on the plane. Maybe something would appeal to me. We let a nurse know where we'd be in case anyone came looking for us.

Clint ordered a cheeseburger, fries, and soda, and I got a fruit cup. We found a table in an empty corner and settled in. As much as I didn't want to get into a heavy conversation on the heels of deciding to take our dad off life support, I knew this would likely be my only time alone with Clint. I launched in.

"It's good to see you," I began. "It's been a long time."

He looked at me like he knew where this was leading.

"Yeah," was all he said. He bit into his burger.

I moved forward anyway. "I'm sorry we . . . drifted apart," I said.

He nodded and wiped the corner of his mouth with a napkin.

"We didn't exactly *drift*," he said.

Ouch. Obviously, he wasn't going to make this easy. I wanted to make amends, but we'd both played a part in our division.

I picked at a piece of watermelon with my plastic fork.

"Well, I'm sorry," I said again, this time truly meaning it as an apology.

He nodded and took another bite.

"How often have you seen him over the years?" I asked, changing the subject to a less confrontational one.

His shoulders relaxed a bit. He shrugged. "A few times. A couple times in Sheboygan, and then last year in Appleton." He took a bite of his burger, and I waited for him to chew and swallow, eager for him to tell me more.

"We picked him up at The Salvation Army, and he took us on a tour of the place." He wiped his mouth with his napkin. "It was depressing, but he seemed really happy to be there—like it was the best place he'd been in a while."

I shook my head. How terribly sad.

"We played pool for a while and then took him to a doctor's appointment he'd told us he had. We planned to go to the Oneida Casino afterward. But then—this was weird—when he got out of the doctor's office, he was surprised to see us waiting for him. I mean, of course we were waiting for him. We'd travelled to see him. Why would he think we'd ditch him?"

"That *is* weird," I agreed.

"It happened again when we were at the casino." He stopped eating, fully engaged. "We gave him some money to play with, and he played slots while we played Blackjack, so we didn't see him for a while. But each time we'd go find him to meet back up, he'd say, 'Oh, I thought you guys left.' He must've said it like five or six times. Maybe he thought we'd want to pay him back by leaving him like he'd left us."

I gave my brother a skeptical look. My dad's actions surprised me as much my brother's reasoning for them. I pushed my fruit cup away and continued listening.

"What sucks now," Clint said, "is that I have no answers. I

should've asked the questions I wanted to ask. I should've taken advantage of the opportunities to talk with him, but I didn't, and I won't ever get to again."

I nodded and took a deep breath, wishing I could lessen his pain. "I get that."

I felt a similar ache for not having done more the past seven years. The division that existed between me and my dad seemed so senseless now that we were at the end.

Would I have done more if I'd known he was homeless? Would I have tried harder if I'd viewed alcoholism as a disease rather than a flaw in his character? Maybe attending an Al-Anon meeting would've helped me better understand his behavior. Instead, I gave him the space I thought he desired and built a wall to protect myself from the pain his absence produced.

Clint finished his burger and took a sip of his soda.

"Ya know, for years I wondered who this guy was," he said. "I wondered if the little bit my mother had told me about him was true. Then I finally got to meet him, and he didn't have as much to say to me as I would've thought. After not seeing me for fourteen years, I'd expected more, but he was so quiet. Then again, I was quiet, too. I should've said more. I should've gone to see him more. I just thought I'd have more time."

I looked into his sweet face, the face that looked so much like our dad's, and I wished they could've known each other better. They were alike not just in stature and eye and hair color. They were alike in spirit, in the way they related to people, and in the gentle way they spoke. There was a certain kindness and easiness about them. If they'd had more time to get to know each other, I think they would've really liked each other.

"About that other stuff," Clint said, "I see it like this—Cliff and I grew up with a sort of 'street mentality,' and we thought you were on our side. We trusted you. So when you told Erin what was going on with Cliff, it felt like you crossed us."

It took a few seconds for that to sink in.

"I can see that," I said. For a moment, I wished I could go back and do it differently.

"I was young and stupid. I'm sorry, too." Clint picked up a french fry and held it out to me, like a peace offering.

I laughed and accepted it, thinking our dad would've done something just like that to lighten the mood.

We headed back to the waiting room on the third floor. Cliff was just coming back from our dad's room when we arrived. A look passed from him to Clint.

You're up, little brother, it said.

Clint nodded at him, gave me a smile, and then headed to the nurse standing by. He'd never get all the answers he wanted, but maybe at least he'd take this opportunity to ask the questions and to say what he needed to say.

"You wanna go for a walk?" Cliff asked before I sat down.

I sure did. Just as with Clint, this would likely be our only chance to talk privately, and I wanted to know how he was feeling, both in the moment and about being back in jail. Why had he resorted to selling weed? Where were his children? I was eager to hear anything he was willing to share.

CHAPTER 32
No Perfect Crime

I let a nurse at the station know Cliff and I would be back shortly. We'd have to be—it was just past four o'clock, and Tara would be arriving soon, not to mention the chaplain might be looking for us.

I followed Cliff down the hallway, noting the clothes that hung from his frame—a bulky white sweatshirt three times his size and a baggy pair of blue jeans. Was that what he'd been wearing when he got arrested in July, or had Clint brought him clothes to change into? It was odd to think he'd come straight from jail that morning, and he'd go back there tonight. No comforts of home would greet him. Even his time was no longer his own.

We arrived at the cafeteria, but Cliff wasn't interested in eating. We found a table away from the crowd and he plunked down across from me. He looked older than his twenty-five years. His pale complexion reminded me he'd hardly seen the sun in six months.

Our eyes locked, and I told myself to shut up so he could speak first.

He laid his hands flat on the table between us and leaned toward me.

"I fucked up," he said. He sat still and stared into my eyes.

It wasn't what I'd expected to hear, but it was a good place to start.

I could feel the vibration of his leg shaking nervously under the table. He tapped his fingers and went on to tell me *how* he'd fucked up, that he *hated* he'd fucked up, and that he was *never* gonna fuck up again. When he finished, his shoulders slouched forward, and his chin dropped to his chest.

I felt the same lurch in my heart as I had with Clint, the same longing to take away his pain.

"Why did you do it?" I asked gently. I knew how hard he'd worked to stay "legit," but my guess was he wanted fast cash, and he knew how to get it.

"Minimum wage sucks!" He sat up and pressed his fingers to his forehead. "I tried. I really did, but I couldn't keep up. There were so many court costs—for my past actions and to get custody of the kids. It was all so much."

I nodded. He'd shared that struggle with me before, back when he'd been living at Sarah's and he'd had even less to pay for. He looked down and slowly shook his head.

The previous time he'd gone back to jail, he'd written to me that it would be the last time.

I'm missing out on too much, he'd said, *on the kids and life in general. Each time I get locked up, I think, "I know the perfect crime for when I get out." But each time I'm out, my "perfect crime" locks my ass back up!*

After ten long years, I conclude that there is no perfect crime. And it's not worth it. I can live a nice, normal life. I will do it, too.

Now, slouched in front of me, head down, he was a picture of regret.

"How did you get caught?" I asked. If he'd expected this to

be a "perfect crime," getting arrested would surely have been a shock.

His eyes narrowed. "A guy I sold weed to was wearing a wire."

I wanted to say I was sorry, but I wasn't sorry he got caught. I was sorry he'd decided to do it. Sorry he'd lost everything because of it. I'd been hopeful that he was through with all of that, that the cycle he'd learned about in his psychology classes had finally been broken. He'd been free. I hated that he wasn't anymore. And then there were his children to think about.

"Where are your kids?" They were now five and six years old. I hoped they were with Margaret.

Cliff's eyes fell. "In foster care. I was supposed to get full custody—but then this." He said there'd been a court date set for Erin to give up her rights, but he'd gone back to jail before that could happen.

It was crushing to hear that he'd come so close to keeping them, only to lose them once more.

"I had thirty days to sign over guardianship, so Margaret and her husband did a thirty-day foster program so they can be the foster parents. She kept hinting that I could sign over my rights. They're trying to get Erin's rights terminated, too. They wanna keep the kids."

He tapped his fingers on the table again. I wanted to take them in my hands, to calm him, but I didn't want to stop him from working through his grief. From releasing his anger and sharing his disappointment.

I knew his losing custody of his children was the worst error he could've possibly made. Margaret and her husband had been wonderful, and they would likely be the perfect foster parents for his son and daughter, but he was their biological father, and he knew he had failed them—just as his biological father had failed him.

He lifted his face and looked into my eyes as if he was trying to read my thoughts.

Was he afraid that I thought less of him? That I didn't love him anymore or thought what he'd said about trying to improve his life had been bullshit?

In years past, he would have thought all those things. His unexpected visit to Charlotte five years earlier had shaken our foundation. In a letter written shortly afterwards, he'd shared, *I often wonder what kind of relationship we're supposed to have . . . I'd like to have a close relationship, but I felt it wasn't possible because of my past actions. Like you regretted meeting me and wanted to blow me off nicely.*

But we'd come so far since then. We'd written dozens of letters and had many long phone calls, talking about life and the things that really mattered. As I looked across the table at him, I hoped that all he saw was love and understanding and sympathy.

"I'm so sorry," I said and reached out to him. His fidgeting had stopped, and I took his hands in mine.

"I lost my kids."

"I know, honey. But you're gonna get out, and you can still have a relationship with them. You can get another job, and you can do it all over again. You know you can because you did it already."

He looked at me doubtfully.

"I'm proud of all the things you did right." I squeezed his fingers.

He stared hard into my face. "I'm *never* gonna fuck up again."

I smiled. "I know," I said.

We walked back to the waiting room and found it empty. It was four-thirty. I hoped Clint would get back before Tara, Peggy, and the chaplain arrived, so I'd have more time to be alone with my dad. I peered out the window and waited. Cliff took a seat, leaned back, and closed his eyes.

Clint was back within minutes. He gave me a nod and a smile that I took to mean he'd done what he'd wanted to.

"Okay, then," I said, deciding my brothers were okay at the moment, that I could go see our dad alone for what might be the last time. "I'm gonna go back in for a little while. When Tara gets here, come get me."

Clint said he would. Cliff didn't open his eyes. I walked out of the waiting room and approached a nurse standing by.

"You can go ahead," she said, motioning down the hall toward my dad's room.

"Oh, I . . ."

There would be no nurse's shoes to follow this time. I glanced down at my own shoes and a song lyric from a classic Christmas movie came to mind. *Just put one foot in front of the other.*

It would be okay.

CHAPTER 33
Blue-Eyed Groupie

Upon arriving at the door to my dad's ICU room, it struck me how much I'd learned about him since my last visit just a few hours before. I had a better picture of what his life had looked like during the past several years. More importantly, I knew more about his accident and injuries. And because of what I'd learned, I'd made the decision, along with my brothers, to end his life support.

I took a deep breath to steady myself and walked in.

My dad looked no different than before. He still showed no signs of distress.

I'd made the right decision, hadn't I? *His brain cannot be repaired*, I reminded myself. He looked fine, but I knew he was not.

I moved along the railing at the side of his bed, stopping at the same spot where I'd stood before, next to his uncovered hand. I scanned his body for any signs of life other than the rise and fall of his chest aided by machines. His face seemed frozen in time. His limbs didn't move.

My dad is going to die tonight.

Tears pricked my eyes. I reached for his fingers and held them in mine. I'd never known just when he might show up in my life, but now I knew he never would again.

I was grateful for this moment to hold his hand—such a simple connection, yet so powerful. I was here, and we were together, one last time.

In the stillness of the room, the whirring of the machines caught my attention just as they had before. It was a miracle what those machines could do, breathing for my dad and sending oxygen to his organs. For that matter, it was a miracle that my dad had made it to the hospital. He could've died when his head hit the windshield. He could've died face down on the pavement. But because he'd held on long enough to get to Froedtert, and because of these amazing machines, I'd been able to come and be with him. So had Cliff and Clint. And soon, Tara would be here as well. Thanks to those miracles, all four of us had this time with him.

For me, this was the end of a long, difficult road. But what I thought of now, as I held his fingers and felt the warmth of his skin next to mine, were the happy memories, that ones that had always put a smile on my face. I told him about them now—how I loved watching the Eighth Street Bridge open and sitting on Grandma's porch swing and listening to him play guitar.

I named off all the songs I remembered him singing and told him how I especially loved "The Cover of the Rolling Stone" because I'd sung backup on that one.

"You'd sit on your stool, and I'd stand next to you," I said, talking to him as if he could hear me. I had to believe he could. "You'd adjust the mic just right so we could both sing into it."

My favorite line, I told him, was the one about the "blue-eyed groupies" because that's how I saw myself in relation to him. I'd been born with blue eyes, just like he had, and they'd turned green over time, but I was still his blue-eyed groupie. I was his biggest fan.

I told him corny things I remembered him saying, like "The blind man picked up his hammer and *saw*."

I told him I was glad he'd come to my high-school graduation and that I still read my horoscope sometimes and that Larry had bought me a guitar for Christmas one year because I'd given away the one I got for my tenth birthday, and I wanted to learn to play again.

I told him I was grateful he'd hung on after the accident. That I was grateful for this time with him. Grateful to be able to say goodbye in person.

"But I'm not saying goodbye right now," I said. "Tara is coming, and I'll be back with her."

I glanced at my watch. It was almost five. Had she already arrived? Had she met Cliff and Clint in the waiting room? Maybe she still wasn't here. Maybe something had happened on the way. Had she even left Sheboygan yet?

"I'll be back," I told my dad, and I let go of his hand. "I'm gonna go check on her."

I left his room and made my way back to the waiting area. Cliff and Clint were standing by the window talking when I arrived.

"Is Tara here?"

They turned to look at me. Clint flipped up his palms, emphasizing that the room was empty.

"She'd said they'd be here around four." I moved past them to look out the window and peered down into the lit parking lot, as if by chance I'd see her walking up.

"Miss Wilsing?" A voice came from behind me. I spun around, expecting to see a nurse standing in the hallway, hoping she'd escorted Tara to us. Instead, I saw an unfamiliar woman in an emerald blouse and black dress pants. She greeted me with a warm smile.

"My condolences," she said in a pleasant voice.

Cliff and Clint came to my side.

"I didn't want to disturb you while you were with your father," the woman continued. "My name is Chantel, and I'm with the Wisconsin Donor Network."

My hand went to my heart. Cliff put his arm around my shoulders. Clint reached for my other hand.

Chantel continued talking, but I missed half of what she said as my mind processed the word "donor."

"Do you know if your dad is registered with us?"

I regained enough focus to answer. "No, I don't."

"Well," she said, "we can see if he's in the system—and if not . . . if you're interested . . ."

I looked at her wide-eyed. I'd barely processed the decision we'd made to remove life support. I'd just begun to come to terms with his dying. I hadn't given any thought to what we'd do with his body once his soul had left it.

I was being asked now to decide that, too.

I took a moment to gather my thoughts. I couldn't think of any reason we wouldn't want to do this. He'd be gone; his organs might help others. Something good could come of all this. It made sense to me.

I looked to my brothers and could see the slight nods of their heads. We seemed to all be thinking the same thing. I nodded as well.

Chantel watched and waited for my response.

"That would be wonderful," I said finally.

She gave us a solemn smile. "Thank you," she said. "We're deeply grateful."

I let her know we were waiting on our sister and a friend of the family, as well as the chaplain, before removing life support. She said she'd return later. There'd be papers to fill out and tests to run to ensure he was a viable candidate.

She turned to leave, and I watched as she headed down the

hallway. Over her shoulder, I happened to catch a glimpse of a young, attractive blonde woman walking straight toward me, a huge smile breaking on her face, a young man at her side.

I smiled back and waved my arms, overjoyed. My baby sister had arrived.

CHAPTER 34
A Few Steps Away

"I found you!" Tara threw her arms open wide and hugged me. Jake was at her heels, and the chaplain was right behind him. I hugged her back, said hello to Jake, and greeted the chaplain while trying to introduce everyone to each other.

Cliff and Clint joined us, and I turned to the chaplain to ask if we could please have some time. He could see that Tara had just arrived, and I let him know we needed to catch her up and tell her the decision we'd made after talking with the doctors. She also would need some time with our father.

"Certainly." He said it in a way that made me feel like we could take all the time in the world. "Just let the nurse know when you're ready. I'm here all night." And with that, he left us.

I introduced Cliff, Clint, and Tara to each other, just as I'd always hoped to. They turned to face each other, scanning and searching for similarities and differences. Clint and Tara were taller and thinner than Cliff and me. They had blue eyes, and we had green. Their hair was blonder than ours. But our skin tones matched exactly, and you could see a part of our dad in each of our faces. The four of us stood just smiling at each other. We'd done it. We were together—for the first time ever.

Tara turned to welcome Jake into our circle. He'd stepped aside to give us a moment. We all shook hands, and he apologized for arriving later than we'd expected.

"Work ran long," he said.

"It's all good," I said, and I meant it. I didn't care that they were late. I felt blessed beyond measure.

Cliff, Clint, and I updated Tara and Jake on our dad's condition and told them of our decision to take him off life support. Tara bowed her head, Jake took her hand, and I continued.

"We requested the chaplain who followed you in, and we've been asked about organ donation."

"Organ donation?" She lifted her head and looked at me through bleary eyes.

"Yeah, I know," I said. "It's a lot to take in."

Tara had written letters to me religiously since she'd first learned how to write, but there hadn't been one letter in all those years that had mentioned our dad. And the brief conversation we'd had two years earlier while kayaking in the ocean had been the last time I'd brought him up.

Clint handed her a tissue and she dabbed under her eyes.

She'd never truly get to meet him. That seemed to be sinking in.

Perhaps she'd come thinking it was mostly for my benefit, or she'd been motivated by the chance to meet Cliff and Clint. But maybe now she was realizing she needed something for herself.

"Do you want to see him alone?" I put my hand on her shoulder. "Or should we all go together?"

Her eyes widened and she blinked a few times. "Let's go together."

The five of us walked into the hallway where a nurse let us

know it was okay to go to his room. The way was familiar to me now, and on this—my third visit—I didn't even have to take a deep breath before entering.

We walked in, and I returned to my usual spot, near his hand. Tara stood next to me, with Jake to her right. Cliff and Clint went to the opposite side of the bed.

There we were—the four of his children—together with him for the first time ever.

For a few seconds, no one said a word. Then Tara broke the silence. "I went to see him a couple of months ago."

I was shocked—both that she'd gone and that she hadn't told me.

Her words hung in the air. No one moved. My head was down, my eyes focused on our dad.

"I decided it was time," Tara continued. "I tracked him down to his friend's house in Sheboygan."

We all stayed silent.

"I was on the front porch, just a few steps away from the door."

I stole a glance in her direction. She was staring straight ahead as if in a trance. Lost in the memory.

"I couldn't bring myself to knock." Her chin dropped to her chest, and her long blond bangs fell across her face. "I just couldn't do it."

Her voice became a whisper. "I wish I had."

Oh, Tara. I wanted to hold her and tell her that everything was going to be okay, but no amount of comforting would take away that ache.

Jake reached for Tara's hand, and she turned to hug him.

"Do you want some time alone in here?" I asked.

With her head buried in Jake's shoulder, she nodded yes.

Jake stayed with her while Cliff, Clint, and I made our way back to the ICU waiting room. Someone had been there in our absence, and *Wheel of Fortune* was playing on the television that

I hadn't even noticed was in the room. I tried to guess a word puzzle but found myself thinking about Tara. I walked back to my dad's room.

Jake was sitting on the floor outside the door when I arrived. His head rested against the wall. I slid down next to him, and we talked about how Tara was feeling. How sad she was that she was meeting her dad for the first time, here, like this. And how glad she was that we were all here. She emerged from the room wiping away tears from her eyes, and we stood up. She was surprised but grateful to find me there. She fell into my arms and then into Jake's.

We went back to the waiting room. Cliff and Clint each wanted to go back to our dad. Clint went first.

I wanted to go to the lobby to wait for Peggy. It was almost seven o'clock, and I expected she would arrive any minute. Tara and Jake went with me.

We'd no sooner gotten there when Peggy strolled in. Dressed in a sparkly holiday sweater, with a jingle bell hanging from a thin cord around her neck and jingle bell earrings to match, she looked like Christmas cheer itself. She spotted me and headed in our direction.

I eyed the large red container she was carrying. It was decorated with a band of white snowflakes.

"I went to a cookie exchange last weekend," she said, shifting the container to one arm so she could hug me with the other. "And I can't eat them all by myself!" She laughed and then gave Tara a hug, too. "It's good to see you again." They'd met just once, six years earlier at my wedding. Peggy had been my maid of honor.

Tara introduced her to Jake.

Peggy cracked open the lid of the container and tilted it toward us. The aroma of the sweet, buttery scents overwhelmed me, and I reached in and selected a green frosted sugar cookie dotted with Red Hots. If ever I needed comfort food, this was it, and what could be more comforting than a homemade Christmas cookie offered by my oldest, dearest friend? I gave Peggy another hug. Not only had she come to be by my side, she'd brought Christmas joy along with her.

I'd just taken my first bite when I heard my maiden name once again.

"Miss Wilsing?" It had come from behind me.

Turning with my mouth full, I encountered a slender young man holding a clipboard.

"I'm Eric. With the Wisconsin Donor Network. Chantel said you were willing to talk with us."

I swallowed my bite and nodded.

"Thank you," he said. "Please follow me."

Peggy closed the lid and looked at me questioningly. I caught her up as Eric led the four of us out of the lobby and into an expansive, softly lit sitting room. Cushy couches lined the edges, and eight overstuffed chairs formed a circle in the center. We each chose to sit in one of those, facing each other, Eric included.

"Chantel will be here in a minute with your brothers and the chaplain." He smiled and then scribbled something on the pages clipped to his board.

I looked around the room for clues as to how this all might work. There would be questions for us, I assumed, but I didn't know if we'd have any answers. All I knew was that my dad had been an alcoholic and a smoker for most of his life, and that gave me zero confidence that he'd be a viable organ donor.

Please, I sent my prayer out into the universe, *let us have this one thing. Let his death offer hope to others.*

CHAPTER 35
Each Little Box

There were very few things I knew about organ donation. When I was sixteen and applying for my driver's license, I'd checked *yes* when asked if I'd be a donor because it seemed like the obvious thing to do. If others could benefit, why would I say no? But I'd never thought about how it would actually happen.

I'd read news stories about transplants and had heard of people being on waitlists, but I didn't know anyone who'd gone through the process. And of course, I'd never been asked to make the decision for someone else.

"When there's no evidence of a person's wishes, such as the case here," Chantel began, "the legal next of kin is authorized to give consent. Do you give consent?"

I nodded my head. "I do." I felt the same way I'd felt at sixteen. It was the right thing to do.

Chantel solemnly smiled. "Thank you," she said.

Peggy placed her hand on the armrest of my chair, giving me silent reassurance that she was there for me. Cliff looked to Clint, seated beside him, and Tara reached out to Jake. The chaplain, who'd chosen to stand, padded around the room.

"To determine if your dad is a medically viable donor," Chantel continued, "we need to ask a list of questions and run some tests on your father. Will that be all right?"

I looked to Cliff and Clint, and we all nodded yes.

"We'll start with your options," Eric said, "the list of organs that can be donated."

There were those I'd expected to hear—his heart, kidneys, pancreas, and eyes, and those I'd never thought of—his skin, bones, and veins. And then there was the one I assumed wouldn't be viable because of his alcoholism—his liver. We approved them all.

We consented to his organs being used for transplants and for medical and dental research and education.

Eric handed me his clipboard and a pen and asked me to sign the authorization form. I scanned the page we'd just completed. *In order that humanity may benefit*, it read, *this anatomical gift is made of or from the body of <u>ROY WILSING</u> after death.* Eric had written our dad's name in blocky capital letters. I stared at it, thinking again how surreal this whole experience was. Then I glanced at the checklist below where Eric had marked all our choices. Each little box represented a piece of our dad's body.

It was strange to contemplate the dismantling of it. How miraculous it was that we humans had learned our parts could be taken from one and given to others.

I signed the page and handed the board back to Eric. He signed below me, as a witness to my wishes, then looked to the four of us—me, Cliff, Clint, and Tara—sitting across from him in birth order from left to right.

"Do you know if your dad had been seen by a physician or been hospitalized in the past two years?"

I looked to Cliff, now knowing he and Clint had taken our dad to an appointment.

"Yeah," Cliff said. "When we met him in Appleton last

year, he asked us to take him to a doctor's office before we went to a casino."

It was odd to think they'd seen him without me—not just then but every time they'd been together. They'd had their own relationship with him, outside of me.

"Do you know where he went or what he went for?"

"Back pain, I think," Cliff answered. He looked to Clint for confirmation.

"Yeah, back pain," Clint said. "We took him and waited for him."

"He broke his back in 1975," I added, remembering the song I'd made up about his back brace. It seemed my only contribution to this conversation would be what had happened long ago.

The chaplain was now moving silently around the outside of our chairs, encircling us as if he were forming an invisible, protective shield. I felt free to take all the time we needed for this very important discussion.

Eric scribbled down some notes and then resumed asking the questions on the form. We did our best to answer what we could.

There were no major illnesses or surgeries that we knew of. No known allergies or history of sexually transmitted diseases. No recent sickness. No recent travel.

He looked up, pen poised in his hand. "What was his occupation?"

"He laid flooring," Cliff and I said in unison, surprising each other.

Eric nodded and wrote it down. He said my Aunt Eunice had told a nurse about our dad's history with tobacco products. Someone must have called her to ask questions as well. "She said he started in his teens. At least a pack a day was her guess."

I nodded. That sounded right. "For probably forty years," I

said. I'd never known him to go a day without his Viceroys, though I'd tried to convince him to quit when I was a child. I'd even hidden his pack of cigarettes a few times.

"And alcohol?" Eric asked. I was sure Aunt Eunice had told them about that, too.

Cliff, Clint, and I looked at each other.

"How much? If you had to guess."

It was hard to say. "Maybe a twelve-pack a day?" I offered. "Since his mid-thirties, maybe earlier."

Eric wrote it down and asked about our family history of illnesses.

Grandpa Wilsing had diabetes, I told him. He hadn't changed his lifestyle and died from it in his early seventies. My uncles—our dad's three older brothers—all died before the age of sixty from different types of cancer. The oldest of the three had died first, at the age of fifty-one.

The odds of our dad being a viable donor weren't looking great.

Was there any history of heart disease? Or kidney disease? High blood pressure? Chest pain?

Not that I knew of. I looked to Cliff and Clint. They didn't know either.

Poor circulation? Digestive issues? Asthma? Glaucoma?

No one knew. Not just no one in the room, but no one anywhere that we knew of. He was the only one with the answers to these questions, and that inescapable fact brought to light just how alone he really must've been.

And for how many years? I pressed my hand to my heart, as if pushing on it could ease the ache I felt.

Jake reached for the tissue box on the table behind him and handed a few to Tara. She'd been silent throughout the questioning. She sniffled and dabbed at her eyes. I realized that while Cliff, Clint, and I were learning some new details about our dad, she was learning many things for the first time.

How terribly sad it was to know this was her formal introduction to him.

"We were told he's lived in shelters or with friends for the past ten years," Eric said. "With his last known residence being The Salvation Army. Does that sound correct?"

Ten years? I thought back to my visit with him seven years earlier, when he'd been living upstairs from a friend. I remembered now that he'd said his friend had been letting him stay there. I'd assumed he'd been paying rent. Maybe he hadn't been.

Ten years back meant he'd been living that way since 1993, the year before I'd called him from my weekend course. That would explain why he hadn't reached out to me during that time. Maybe he'd been focused on just trying to survive.

"Yes," I said. "That sounds correct."

Cliff and Clint nodded in agreement, knowing he'd definitely lived at the shelter for a couple of years.

"Thank you," Eric said. He added that any "high-risk" details—*much of our dad's profile must've fit that description*—would be communicated to the physicians who were offered the organs for their patients.

"We'll be running several tests," Chantel said, "to check the viability of each one."

I hadn't known they could do that, but it made sense.

"And they'll scan his skin to determine if there are any signs of skin cancer," Eric said.

The thought of our dad's body being further examined was unsettling given all we knew he'd been through, but if those tests determined he was a viable candidate—if even just one part of him could be given to someone in need—it would be worth it.

"You can wait for the results in here or go back to the ICU waiting room on the third floor," Chantel said. She and Eric rose from their seats. "The nurses will find you when we know more. It shouldn't take too long. Maybe an hour."

Upon their exit from the room, Cliff, Clint, Tara, and I rose as well, each of us emotionally exhausted after the hour-long meeting. We stood and stretched, and then—as if pulled together by an invisible force in the room—we moved to the center of the circle, found each other's arms, and embraced in our first family hug.

No one spoke for a few moments. It was enough—it was everything—to be together on this day.

The chaplain stood nearby. "In my eight years at this hospital," he said tenderly, "this is the most overwhelming situation I've ever seen."

We dropped our arms and turned to him. Peggy came to my side, and Jake went to Tara's.

"I'm so sorry," the chaplain said to her, "for you having to meet your father like this—for the first time, on his deathbed. And for meeting your brothers for the first time under these circumstances."

She gave him a sad smile and used her wadded-up tissue to wipe her nose.

He turned to me. "If it's all right, I'd like to stay with you while you wait."

"That would be nice," I said. We'd hardly spoken since I'd requested him hours earlier, but it felt right that he should be with us.

"I went to your father's room earlier today to share with him some words of encouragement. I prayed for him and said a blessing."

I smiled through the tears that came to my eyes, so grateful for his kindness.

"We could go together right now if you like—to pray for him—while you're waiting for the test results." He looked at our assembled group. "We could all go."

I looked to Cliff, Clint, and Tara. They slowly nodded yes, likely imagining, as I was, what it would be like. All of us gathered together with our dad. To pray for him. To say goodbye. Were we ready?

"Are you okay to stay?" I asked Cliff. It was just after eight o'clock. If he stayed, he'd get back to jail later than his twelve-hour pass allowed, but I couldn't imagine him not being with us.

"Yeah, it's okay," he said. "I'll call them." He gave me a reassuring nod. "Let's go."

We followed the chaplain out of the room in pairs. Peggy beside me, holding my hand. Jake and Tara behind us, and Cliff and Clint at the end.

"We need to drive back tonight," Tara whispered to me as we traveled down the hallway. "We can't stay too late."

I nodded that I understood. "I'm so glad you're here," I said. "Just stay however long you can."

We arrived outside our dad's door, and as the chaplain turned the handle, the weight of the moment hit me.

We were going in to say goodbye.

That was so different from saying hello. So different from sharing my best memories. And even though I had the chaplain to guide me, Peggy to hold my hand, and my brothers and sister gathered by my side—by his side—it still seemed an impossible thing to do. I'd spent so much of my life without my dad, but at least there had always been hope. Now that hope was gone, and it hurt to think of letting him go forever.

CHAPTER 36
The Father Wound

We formed a semicircle around the bed, the chaplain standing where I'd been earlier, near our dad's hand. Tara was at the chaplain's side, and Jake was next to her. I stood on the opposite side of the bed, with Cliff to my right and Clint and then Peggy to my left.

We watched as the chaplain placed his hand on our dad's head, then we took each other's hands and bowed our heads.

"Almighty God, gracious Father," the chaplain began. "Hear our prayers for your servant, Roy Earl Wilsing."

That alone was enough to make me want to cry. He was speaking to God, summoning the Universe, to pay attention to what was happening in that room. To notice our dad in his time of need.

"Comfort him," he continued, "and comfort his children—Gina, Cliff, Clint, and Tara—that they may find joy in the sorrow and laughter in the tears."

My head bowed, my hands in each of my brother's hands, I felt confident that the four of us would find comfort in each other from that day forward. Reconnecting with my brothers had been a gift, and I hoped this time spent together with Tara would mark the beginning of a friendship between her and them.

The chaplain stopped speaking, and I raised my head.

"Do you have any prayers for him?" he said.

Everyone looked up. The chaplain had likely meant that question for all of us, but I felt obligated to speak first—to lead the way, though I didn't know what to say.

I looked at our dad's face, and a calm presence washed over me.

"I pray for your comfort and your rest from this life," I said to him.

At least he'd no longer have to struggle. And if there was a Heaven, surely his whole family would be there to welcome him. His three brothers and his parents would be waiting.

"I wish for peace," I said. "For you and for all of us. I wish us peace in our hearts and minds."

I thanked him for Cliff, Clint, and Tara, and told him that I loved him. It didn't seem like enough to say, but it was all that really mattered.

Clint cleared his throat. "Thank you for bringing me into the world and for giving me life."

I thought of Clint's wish for more time with our dad and his questions that would go unanswered, and tears came to my eyes. I could answer some things for him, and I could share stories and pictures. It wouldn't be enough or replace what he'd missed, but it would be something.

We looked to Cliff, thinking he'd go next. He stared at our dad and shook his head. He looked away and said nothing.

Tara stepped closer to the bed, tears gently rolling down her cheeks. "I never really knew you," she said, "but I love you."

Cliff dropped my hand. "He pissed his life away!" he suddenly spat out.

Everyone turned to look at him. His face reddened, and he clenched his fists as if he wanted to punch something.

I stepped back to give him some space.

"He just pissed it away!" Cliff threw his arms up in the air. Then his tears began to flow. He stomped his foot and turned away from us, sobbing.

The chaplain looked at each of us. "You're feeling 'The Father Wound,' " he said.

In all my months of receiving counseling, I'd never heard that term. But that was exactly what it felt like—a wound. Caused by our father. Each of us had experienced it in a different way. Each of us hurt because of it.

Part of Cliff's anger though, I knew was not directed at our dad. Yes, Cliff wished our dad had made better choices and that they'd had a closer relationship, but I was sure in this moment it wasn't our dad he was most angry with.

I stepped toward him and touched the back of his shoulder. "Learn from him," I whispered. "Don't do the same thing."

He turned his head just slightly in my direction.

"That's what I want for you," I said.

He wiped his eyes with the back of his hand and then, head down, turned in our direction.

"You can stop the cycle, Cliff," the chaplain reassured him. "You can be there for your children."

Cliff looked as vulnerable as a child himself. Using the cuff of his sweatshirt, he wiped his face and tried to compose himself, only to fall into my arms and cry harder. We all stayed silent, allowing him the time he needed to get out his disappointment and anger and to let the chaplain's words sink in.

After several minutes, when Cliff was ready to proceed, we resumed holding hands around the bed and bowed our heads as the chaplain recited Psalm 23, "The Lord is My Shepherd."

He paused before continuing with a prayer.

"Almighty God, look on Roy, whom you made your child in baptism. Comfort him with the promise made by the death and resurrection of your Son, Jesus Christ our Lord."

I saw Tara squeeze Jake's hand. She'd grown up going to church, and I could see this meant something to her. Peggy's eyes met mine, and I knew she was checking in on me, making sure I was okay. I gave her a sad smile. I was so grateful we were together, and it felt so right that the chaplain had joined us. We'd needed the comfort and wisdom he'd given us.

"Roy, our brother in the faith, we entrust you to God who created you. May you return to the one who formed us out of the dust of the earth. Surrounded by the angels and triumphant saints, may Christ come to meet you as you go forth from this life."

I stood with one hand in Cliff's and the other in Clint's, hoping to hold onto this moment in my mind.

This is the last time we'll be with him. There will be no more visits to this room. This is really the end.

"Go forth from this world in the love of God who created you," the chaplain said softly, "in the mercy of Jesus Christ who died for you, in the power of the Holy Spirit who strengthens you, and at one with all the faithful—living and departed. May you rest in peace and rise in the glory of your eternal home, where grief and misery are banished, and light and joy abide. Amen."

"Amen," we repeated in unison. I looked up at the chaplain, who asked if anyone would like to add anything.

We looked around at each other, but no one spoke up.

"Let's have a moment of silence then," he said.

We bowed our heads, and the question crept into my mind, *What would my dad say right now if he could add something?* Would he have told the four of us how much he'd loved us? How happy he was that we were all there? Would he have said he was sorry he'd made such a mess of things?

I lifted my eyes and looked at his face. No, he probably would've told us a joke to lighten the mood, and it would've made us laugh. The thought made me smile.

Others looked up as well, and when it seemed that we were all ready, the chaplain nodded and headed toward the door. Peggy, Jake, and Tara fell in behind him.

Cliff took a last look at our dad and then walked out next to Clint.

I stood at the bed, alone one last time. I kissed my fingertips and touched them to the beige blanket that covered my dad, imagining my love for him flowing through the blanket's fibers and enveloping him. Could he feel it?

Surely, he could.

Go in peace, Dad. I'll always love you.

CHAPTER 37
Even His Liver

The seven of us had just returned to the ICU waiting room when a nurse appeared.

"Chantel is ready to meet with you downstairs," she said. "She has the results of your father's tests."

A fluttering feeling ran through me. I bit the inside of my lip and turned toward my brothers. Did we dare to hope? Clint raised his eyebrows. Cliff shrugged his shoulders.

"Let's go see," he said.

Peggy set down her coat and the red tub of cookies, Jake wrapped his arm around Tara's waist, and together—along with the chaplain, who was still with us—we headed back to the sitting room where we'd met with Chantel and Eric earlier. They stood up as we walked in and invited us to sit once again on the cozy chairs in the middle of the room. The chaplain again declined, choosing instead to pace the floor.

Once we were settled, Chantel began. "All of your father's organs are viable."

I let out a breath I hadn't realized I'd been holding in. She and Eric smiled.

"All of them?" asked Clint. "Even his liver?" His face broke into a silly grin.

I chuckled.

"All of them," she said with a smile.

"That's so wonderful!" I stood, suddenly giddy, and opened my arms toward my siblings, signaling it was time for our second family hug of the day. Tara giggled and got up, followed by Cliff and Clint. I was overcome with gratitude. I had my brothers and my sister with me, and our dad's death was going to bring hope to so many.

As our arms fell from each other, I turned back to Chantel and Eric. "So, how does this work?" I asked, taking my seat again.

"Well," said Eric, "we're in the process of matching your father's blood type and body size with possible recipients who are near Froedtert. And a national search is being done as well."

I felt warm all over. Tara's face was beaming, her blue eyes shining through tears of joy. Peggy came up behind me and gave me a hug.

Cliff cleared his throat. "When will they take him off life support? Will we go back to the room for that?"

The thought of watching our dad slowly slip away was heartbreaking, but I'd be there if we were allowed.

"He'll go to the operating room," Chantel explained. "The nurses will begin prepping him soon. That'll take a couple of hours. Eric and I will stay with him during that time."

I hadn't expected we'd see our dad again, but now we knew for sure. Our time with him was truly over.

"What happens then?" I leaned back in my chair. Peggy stayed by my side.

"The doctors will remove the ventilation system," Eric said. "Once he fails to breathe, move, or show any response to stimulation, he'll be considered brain dead. Patients with a severe neurological injury, like your father, typically progress to brain death rather quickly." He said this was called a "beating-heart organ donation," and it provided the best chance to maximize the number and condition of organs for transplantation. He explained that after our dad's heart stopped beating—after he stopped breathing—a surgeon would step in.

"The advantage of him being in the OR," Chantel explained, "is that doctors can see the vitals of his organs and tell if they're stable and functioning before transplanting them to an ailing patient. This is a tremendous gift for everyone involved."

I looked into the sweet faces of my siblings. Cliff smiled. Clint nodded. And Tara reached for Jake's hand.

I imagined the hospital staff preparing operating tables and workers from the Wisconsin Organ Network filling coolers with ice. Who would the lucky recipients be? Who would get our dad's blue eyes? Who would get his heart?

"What will happen to him when all of that is over?" I could feel everyone's eyes on me, but it was a practical question, and I needed to know.

"That's up to you," Chantel said in my direction. "A nurse will talk with you before you leave so you can let her know your family's wishes."

Our family's wishes. There it was again. How disconcerting it'd been to hear that phrase just two days before when Nurse Sally had asked for me to think about them. Now, it brought me comfort. I wasn't alone anymore. The four of us were now connected and beginning to feel like a family.

"As far as organ donation affects things," Chantel continued, "all options are still available. The decision to donate doesn't interfere with viewings or burial arrangements."

That was hard to believe.

"And is there a cost for any of this?" I vaguely remembered her saying earlier that there wasn't, but I wanted to be sure.

"No, everything's paid for by an organization called Gift of Life. A donor's family doesn't pay for any expenses related to the procedure."

Incredible. I hoped the hospital bill was covered as well. And what about a burial and funeral arrangements? Surely someone would say that would fall to me.

"I'll make you a copy of our records from today," Eric said. "And once we know about organ matches and transplantations, you can call any time to get information on the recipients."

"Oh, that's great," Tara piped in. "It would be so good to know who he helped."

"We have a system of procedures in place for that," Chantel said.

I could hardly believe this was happening. What a blessing.

Chantel and Eric walked us out and wished us well. It was a comfort to know they'd be with our dad until he went to the operating room. We thanked them for everything and told them we looked forward to hearing from them once the procedure was over.

Peggy, Tara, and Jake headed to the ICU waiting room to grab their belongings, including the container of Christmas cookies that Peggy had left behind. Cliff, Clint, and I went to the lobby. They took a seat, and I went to the registration desk to find out my next step. It was nearly ten o'clock, and we'd been at the hospital for what seemed like a week. If there was nothing more I needed to do, I was ready to leave.

I gave the woman behind the counter my name. "I don't know what I need to do next. Do I check out? Do I owe anything?" I held my breath as she retrieved our dad's file, expecting that surely, as next of kin, I would be responsible for something. He had no insurance, I knew that too. My chest tightened as I watched her flip through the papers. Finally, she looked up and gave me a small smile.

"He's a ward of the state," she said.

I'd only ever heard of children being described as that. "What does that mean?"

"It means the State will pay for all his medical expenses."

My mouth fell open, and an audible breath escaped.

Oh, thank God.

But then another thought struck me.

"What about when he passes? What happens then?" I didn't want to come right out and ask if I'd have to pay for a funeral or a burial. That would sound ridiculous. Of course I'd have to pay for those things. He was my dad. He wasn't the hospital's responsibility.

The woman looked back at the papers. "Since he's a ward of the state, that will be taken care of as well."

I blinked at her in disbelief. "Okay—" My shoulders relaxed.

"Although—" She squinted at a page in the file, and I braced myself, expecting her to tell me some exception to the rule.

"They won't cover a funeral or burial." She looked up at me. "The only option is cremation."

I sighed in relief. Cremation was perfect. There'd be no burial. There'd be no need for a funeral.

"That'll be good," I said. I wrote my home address on the form she gave me. His remains would be sent to me.

She went to a back room and returned with my suitcase. "Try to get some sleep," she said, rolling it to me. "We'll call you when there's something to report."

I thanked her and turned to find our group waiting for me in the lobby. The chaplain was talking with Tara.

"I'll watch over your dad," he said as I approached. He reached his hand out to me.

I smiled and took it, imagining him holding our dad's hand —comforting him, praying for him, and preparing him for whatever would come next. "Thank you," I said.

"It was good to have met you all. Take good care of each other." He hugged each of us, gave us a parting nod, and headed toward the elevator.

I assumed everyone except Peggy would head home from the hospital, but to my surprise, no one wanted to leave each other yet. Clint said he was hungry and suggested we find a restaurant. I was hungry, too, and in no hurry to say goodbye. Cliff said he'd already called the jail to let them know things were taking a bit longer than expected, and Tara and Jake were on board to find food. They'd skipped dinner to get to the hospital as soon as possible.

We split up to drive to the restaurant. Peggy took me in her car, and we stopped to check in at our hotel before meeting up with everyone at the all-night Ground Round right next door.

Peggy and I walked in to find my brothers, sister, and Jake at a large table in middle of the otherwise vacant restaurant. Cliff waved us over, as if we wouldn't have found them otherwise, and Clint, Tara, and Jake stopped their conversation to welcome us and quickly went back to talking, pulling us into their discussion.

"Okay," Tara said, "What was one of your most embarrassing moments?"

I laughed and said I'd never tell—but then I did. Each of us did. There were so many stories to share, so much of our lives we'd lived without each other. Now we had the rest of our lives to catch up.

Tara and Clint made plans to see each other soon. "You'll have to drive to Sheboygan until I get a car," she told him. She wrote her phone number and address on a napkin for him.

My heart did a little leap.

"I can take you," Jake volunteered.

He seemed like such a nice guy. I hoped things would work out for him and Tara.

Cliff would return to jail, of course, but Clint said he'd be there for him when he got out. "I love Cliff more than life," he told us, and we could see in his eyes that he meant it.

It was nearly midnight when we decided to leave the restaurant. As much as I didn't want our time together to end, my eyelids were getting heavy, and my brothers and Jake and Tara had an hourlong drive ahead of them.

"We can walk you over to your room," Cliff said as we headed out.

Our group crossed the parking lot in the direction of the hotel. Strolling in the moonlight, I breathed in the sharp chill of the night air, and on my exhale, watched my breath float away in the wind. Sometimes I missed the winters of Wisconsin.

Cliff scooted up next to me and wrapped his arm around my shoulder. "I'm so glad you're all here," I said.

His smile told me he was glad, too.

We got to the room, and Peggy and I invited everyone in to warm up for a minute. She took a seat on one of the two beds. Cliff collapsed into an easy chair, and Clint sat on its armrest and stretched out his legs. Minutes ticked by with hardly a word as we let the day—and this night—settle into our bones.

We'd come to our inevitable goodbye, but nobody wanted to be the one to say it.

When would we all be together again? None of us knew.

"What time does your flight leave tomorrow?" Tara finally asked. She and Jake were sitting on the edge of my bed. I propped up pillows against the headboard and leaned back on them.

"A little after two." Checkout wasn't until eleven o'clock, so

Peggy and I would be able to sleep in before she would take me to the airport around noon.

Cliff rubbed his hands together and got up from his chair. "We'd better get going, I guess." He walked toward me, and Clint followed. Peggy and I got up and hugged them both.

"We'll walk out with you," Jake said. He and Tara rose from my bed and got to the door first.

Cliff and Clint were right behind them.

"Thank you again," I said to Jake. "And everyone, be safe driving home."

I hugged Cliff, then Clint, then Tara—one by one, taking them in, not wanting to let them go.

"I'll call you tomorrow," I said. "When I know something."

Tara nodded, and Jake opened the door.

"I love you all," I said as they walked out.

Cliff turned back one last time and gave me a sweet smile. Then they were gone.

Part Six

CHAPTER 38
Keeping Him Comfortable

DECEMBER 12, 2003

The hotel phone rang, jolting me awake. I opened my eyes to total darkness and for a few seconds didn't know where I was. I fumbled for the receiver on the nightstand, slowly remembering that I was in Milwaukee, in a hotel room with Peggy, and that I was here because my dad was dying.

I whispered hello and found Eric on the line. At the sound of his voice, my eyes went to the digital alarm clock next to the phone. It was 4:15 a.m. Why was he calling so early?

Wait, is everything over? Did my dad pass?

"Your father's made it through an hour of being without care," he said.

My brain tried to make sense of that. "What do you mean?"

Peggy heard me talking and looked out from under her covers.

"After his tubes were removed," Eric said, "he spontaneously began breathing on his own."

"What?" I sat up. "What does *that* mean?"

Peggy sat up in her bed and looked at me, her brows furrowed.

"As far as organ donation is concerned," Eric explained, "the current donations have been canceled."

My hand flew to cover my mouth. *This can't be happening.*

Since the moment I'd learned our dad's organs were viable, I'd felt his donation would give greater meaning to his life. Despite his struggles, in the end, he'd had the opportunity to give renewed life to others. But now, in an instant, that opportunity had vanished. Sorrow washed over me.

Peggy rose and came to sit next to me.

Tears welled in my eyes. *Why?* I wanted to know. I wanted the universe to tell me. *Why couldn't my dad have this one thing?* It wasn't fair.

"I . . ." My voice was hardly above a whisper. I didn't know how to respond.

Eric filled the silence. "There's always a chance of this happening," he said gently.

"If he's breathing on his own . . ." I asked though I didn't want to, "does that mean he could recover?"

Please tell me no. Based on what the doctors had said, it would be a miserable existence. I looked at Peggy and waited for his answer.

"No," Eric said, "he won't recover."

I let out a sigh of relief and shook my head so Peggy would know what he'd said.

"He'll be transferred to Palliative Care. A nurse will talk with you about that shortly. And there's still a slight chance he could be a donor."

"Really? How?"

"After the tubes are removed and a patient is breathing on their own, their organs will retain enough oxygen as long as the patient passes away within twelve hours."

Twelve hours. The tubes had been removed at three o'clock. We had eleven hours to go. Maybe my dad would pass while I was still in Milwaukee.

A nurse came on the line to tell me about Palliative Care. My dad would receive "comfort measures," she said, which I assumed meant morphine. I agreed to a Do Not Resuscitate order.

"He'll be on the fourth floor," she said. "Will you be coming back later this morning?"

My mind spun. I'd had three hours of sleep after one of the most emotional days of my life, and the next day was already dawning. I pictured my dad now, being placed on the operating table, having the tubes removed, the whirring coming to an end. It had to have been a shock to his system to suddenly start breathing again on his own. Had he been aware of it? Was he aware of anything now?

I hadn't prepared myself for the possibility of seeing him again. I'd thought I'd done everything I'd needed to do. How would my heart make it through another visit? Another goodbye?

And yet, how could I not go to him? He was still alive, and I was still here.

"Of course," I heard myself tell the nurse.

I hung up and turned to Peggy. "I have to go back."

She nodded and wrapped me in a hug.

I fell back on my pillow, exhausted and emotionally drained. Peggy climbed back into her bed, and we both managed to sleep for a few more hours. By ten, we were at the hospital being escorted to the Palliative Care wing on the fourth floor, to my dad's new room.

We didn't see the chaplain in the halls, and Cliff, Clint, Tara, and Jake were long gone. I hadn't called anyone to tell them about the failed organ donation. Half of me was still processing the disappointment, and the other half held out hope that it would still happen. I'd wait until I knew more before contacting them.

We arrived at the door, and the nurse walked us in. At first glance, his new room looked like his last one. He was lying still on the bed, but in place of the wondrous machines I'd thought were keeping him alive, there was only a nightstand. And instead of dim lighting, we now had soft rays of sunlight filtering in through a thinly shaded window.

My dad looked the same as well—like nothing had happened since I'd left him, and though I'd been reassured that he wouldn't recover, I couldn't help but wonder, *Why not? If he was breathing on his own, couldn't he continue to do so?*

"We're just keeping him comfortable," the nurse said. She didn't mention any possibility of him surviving. She'd simply said his passing was taking longer than expected. It was just a matter of time. And he could stay until that time arrived.

She left the room, and I took a step toward the end of the bed, with Peggy right behind me.

Without warning, my dad's chest rose, and he let out an explosive cough. His body lunged forward like he was trying to sit up.

I clutched my heart. "Oh, my God!" I turned to Peggy, whose eyes were as wide as mine, and we both looked back at him. His arms were moving erratically, cutting at the space between us. He let out a guttural moan that made it seem as if he was trying to talk to me. I envisioned him sitting up and pointing an accusing finger in my direction.

"How dare you try to get rid of me!" I imagined him saying. "How dare you try to end my life just to make yours easier!"

I pulled my eyes off him and shot over to Peggy.

"No one should have to see this!" I buried my face in her shoulder. "No one should have to see this."

He groaned again, and his arms continued to slice through

the air, making it look as if he could leap out of bed at any second.

I cried out and ran from the room, the image of his flailing arms running through my head.

Peggy found me in the hallway, sobbing. I couldn't stop trembling.

A nurse appeared beside me. She put her arm gently around my shoulders and walked me into a small room—maybe a storage closet—across the hall from my dad's. I leaned against a cold wall and crumpled to the floor where I curled up in a fetal position and wrapped my arms around my knees. My tears kept coming. The pain in my heart wouldn't subside.

How I wished he'd passed away during the night, and my last memory of him could've been our goodbye as a family. How I wished his organ donation had been successful, and I didn't have to hold out hope for another few hours that something might still come of it.

I cried so hard and so long my muscles hurt.

My dad was dying. My dad. And I didn't want to say goodbye to him all over again.

Peggy found me on the floor and slumped down beside me. She took one of my hands in hers but said nothing.

"No one should have to . . ." I muttered between sobs.

The nurse who'd led me to the room peeked in to check on us. Were we okay?

Peggy lit into her. "You're supposed to be keeping him comfortable," she snapped. "He shouldn't be like that!"

The nurse, clearly taken aback, apologized and said she'd tend to him immediately. She left the room.

I stared at Peggy. Since the fifth grade, she'd always been in my corner, but even I was rather shocked by her outburst.

"What?" she said, looking at me with fire still burning in her eyes. "They need to do their job." Her mom had been a head nurse for decades, and Peggy knew what she was talking about.

The abrupt encounter stopped my tears and exhaustion took over. I laid my head on her shoulder, and we sat in silence until I could breathe clearly again.

When we went back into the hall, a different nurse approached us. She led us to a social worker in a nearby room who gave me the phone number of the Sheboygan County coroner's office. They would be handling my father's cremation, she said, and I could call them if I had any questions.

Another nurse stopped in the room to reassure me that they would keep my dad comfortable while also trying to maintain his candidacy as an organ donor. I looked at my watch and saw it was almost eleven o'clock. He would be viable only if he passed away within the next four hours, and I needed to be to the airport by noon.

He was fully sedated now, the nurse said. And of course, still breathing on his own. Would I like to see him once more before leaving to catch my flight?

I closed my eyes and sucked in a breath. If what she said was true—if he was fully sedated—there'd be no more erratic movements. No terrible groaning. No flailing of his arms.

I looked at Peggy, knowing I needed to go.

She nodded. "I'm here if you need me."

The nurse walked me back to his room.

I entered cautiously, praying he was calm.

I could see that he was.

"I'm okay," I told her.

She silently left the room.

Once again, I made my way to his side, disbelieving I was back but grateful for another opportunity to talk to him. His right arm was bent at the elbow, bringing his hand to rest near his face on the pillow behind him. He lay perfectly still, his face tilted to the left, as if he was looking away from me. I heard each shallow, consistent breath he took. I inched closer.

"I love you," I said. I needed to begin with that because next, I had to tell him I was leaving.

It had been different the night before when I'd had no choice but to leave. We weren't allowed in the operating room. We couldn't have stayed and held his hand until the end.

But if he didn't die by three o'clock, if he was no longer a candidate for organ donation, how long would he lie here—with no one by his side? I didn't want my dad to die alone. And yet, it didn't enter my mind to try to stay longer. It'd been hard enough to steal away for just twenty-four hours, and I was needed back home.

Maybe, I thought, in my last minutes with him, I could convince him to let go. If he did, I could hold his hand and be here with him when he passed. He wouldn't have to be alone.

I'd heard that those near death sometimes needed to hear from loved ones that it was okay to leave. If I could ease his pain and my own, it was worth a try.

His eyelids were closed. His chest rose and fell. I started talking.

"I know you've had a hard life, and I want you to know it's okay to go."

There was no movement. No response. I dug deeper. How could I convince him?

"Grandma is waiting for you," I said softly. I imagined her looking down on us and felt the pang of losing her all over again. She *would* be waiting for him though, and she would love having her baby boy with her again "Go to her," I said. "Give her a hug for me." I swallowed hard, knowing that shortly they would both be gone.

"Say hello to Grandpa, too, and Earl and Buddy and Terry. They're all waiting for you."

He didn't budge. He didn't stop breathing.

"You don't need to be here anymore." I was determined to get through to him. "You can rest now."

I felt like a stubborn child. I wasn't getting my way, and I didn't like it. I knew, of course, it was all just wishful thinking. Had it worked, I would've been shocked. Even scared.

Finally, I resigned myself to the idea that he wasn't going to pass while I was there. I pulled a folded piece of paper from my pocket and grabbed a tissue from the box on his nightstand.

"I wrote a note I want to leave with you," I told him, dabbing my eyes. "I'm going to read it to you now."

I took a breath and began. It was a simple note but really all that needed to be said. I planned to ask the nurse to keep it with him until the end—and beyond, if they could.

"We love you, and we always will. We are with you now, and you will always be with us.

Love, Gina, Cliff, Clint, and Tara."

I folded the paper and placed it next to him on the bed. I hoped it could be cremated with him so part of us would always be with him.

His right arm was still crooked at the elbow, his right hand still on the pillow near his face. Taking his fingers in mine, I leaned in and gently kissed the back of his hand. It was so soft. So warm. I could feel the life within him.

"Goodbye," I whispered. I returned his hand to its resting place. "I won't be coming back."

I hated to have say that. I hated to have to leave.

"I'm going to the airport now," I told him. "I'm flying home today."

My insides ached. "I'm so sorry I have to go." I stepped back to take in the sight of him one last time and was planning to leave, but instead blurted out, "You can go, too."

As if in slow motion, his right hand—the one I'd kissed—

rose from the pillow. He let out the deepest of sighs, and his arm fell to his side, landing on my note.

I drew in my breath, watching him a moment longer. Then I walked toward the door, knowing it was okay to leave. He'd heard every word I'd said.

CHAPTER 39
When He Left

DECEMBER 12, 2003

Just twenty-four hours after arriving in Milwaukee, I was buckled into my airline seat for the return trip home. I popped a piece of gum into my mouth and mindlessly chewed. I couldn't get the image of my dad lying alone in his hospital room out of my mind. The nurses would check on him, of course, and the chaplain would likely visit, but no one my dad knew or loved would be there when he left this world.

It should be me.

I tried to shake the regret I felt in having to leave. Had I known I'd be needed, perhaps I would've planned to stay longer. But I hadn't known, and even this short time away from my family had been a challenge.

Had he died during the night, it would've been perfect timing, but this—this was far from ideal. I'd left him to die on his own. I'd have to make do with calling to check on him, and he wouldn't even know I had.

My feet brushed against my carry-on bag lying under the

seat in front of me. My notebook and pen were inside. I reached down, pulled them out, and flipped through the eighteen pages I'd written on the way to Wisconsin. Releasing all those memories from my mind had prepared me for my time at the hospital. Reliving the heartache and remembering the happier times had helped me see my relationship with my dad as a whole.

I turned to the last page I'd written.

I can't believe this is really happening. I keep thinking it's a dream or a long thought in my head about what might happen in the future.

But it was no dream. It had happened. And now I knew how our story ended.

Pen in hand, I turned the page and picked up where I'd left off—how I'd arrived alone, how I'd talked with my brothers, everything we'd done and said, and how I'd felt throughout the day. I drew a stick figure representing our dad on the bed and noted where each of us had stood during prayer time. I jotted down the stories we'd told each other at dinner and the last words I'd said to my dad. I described how his arm had fallen to his side, and how I knew—without a doubt—that he knew I'd been there.

Being with him reminded me of the love I'd known as a child, and I knew now as an adult, that that love would never leave me—neither his for me, nor mine for him.

The pilot announced we were approaching Chicago, my first layover, and I checked the time. It was just after three o'clock. My dad's time as a viable organ donor had run out. I prayed by some miracle there'd be a phone message for me when I got off the plane, giving me the news I was hoping for.

But there was no message.

The finality of this outcome was hard to accept.

I stared hard at my phone. The more I thought about the loss, the more my sadness turned to frustration. Why was the system set up this way? Why couldn't terminal patients be aided in their death so their organs could be viable for others? It wasn't right.

I called Clint and then Tara to update them. Clint felt equally frustrated and said he'd call Cliff. Tara cried, and I told her I'd call her to talk once I was settled back home.

After a second layover, in Charlotte, I arrived in Tallahassee at ten o'clock that Friday night. Our minivan was right where I'd left it the day before. I called the hospital from the parking lot.

My dad was still breathing, the nurse said. There'd been no change.

How could that be? I felt as if I was in an episode of *The Twilight Zone*. How long could my dad hang on? How could he have suffered such trauma and still make it through a whole day on his own?

I started the car and headed for home. As I drove down the familiar streets of Tallahassee, colorful Christmas lights twinkled from rooflines, and inflated snowmen and reindeer dotted my path. I kept the radio off, not yet ready to hear a holiday tune.

Thirty minutes later, I was back in Larry's arms and kissing my children goodnight.

The next afternoon, my mother and Charlie arrived, bringing with them presents, hot cocoa, and candy canes. We'd be celebrating an early Christmas together.

I'd called Froedtert first thing that morning. My dad was resting, they'd said. There were no changes. I gave my mom and Charlie the update, and we talked about my trip.

"There was an article about him in the paper," my mom said. My Aunt Dorothy had told her about it, and we looked it up online.

On Wednesday, December 10, the day after my dad's accident, *The Sheboygan Press* had run the story, "Bicyclist Hurt in Collision with Car." The reporter said my dad was in critical condition and gave the name of the woman whose car he'd crashed into.

Charlie looked over my shoulder as I read the story on the computer.

"I don't know that I'd have gone if I were you," he said.

That didn't surprise me. In all the years Charlie had been in my life, I'd never spoken to him at length about my relationship with my dad. He knew some of the highs and lows, mostly from conversations with my mom, but he didn't know the depth of my love for my dad or the light he'd been in my life during my early years. And though I'd been part of both of their worlds, they'd lived only on the fringes of each other's. Of course he wouldn't understand why I'd felt compelled to go. How could he have?

I called the hospital again Sunday morning. My dad was still breathing.

Monday morning was the same. After my mom and Charlie left that afternoon, it dawned on me that the police would have a report of the accident. I called the station and ordered it.

When I phoned Froedtert Tuesday morning, the nurse who answered said there were no new developments. I felt better now about leaving Milwaukee when I had. When I'd thought he might last only a day or two, I'd felt guilty, thinking I should've figured out how to stay, but we were five days out now. I didn't see how I could've done that.

On my Wednesday call, I learned that though he was hanging on, his body was showing signs of deterioration. His temperature had started to spike, and his lungs were becoming congested.

Why did it have to come to this?

He'd developed aspiration pneumonia, the nurse said.

I looked that up later. It sounded awful, and it made me angry.

Now, not only were his organs deteriorating and useless to others, but he was having to needlessly suffer when it had already been determined that he wouldn't survive. Euthanasia came to mind. *Why isn't that legal everywhere?* Weren't we here to help each other? The way the system was set up, who were we helping?

Thursday morning, I was told there'd been no significant changes, but it was noted that the chaplain had visited him again. It was comforting to know he was checking in, just like he'd said he would.

It had been a week since I'd seen my dad. The lyrics from Don McLean's song "American Pie" ran through my head, and I pictured him in his attic room at Grandma's house singing about the day the music died. It was another of his favorites. I could hear him strumming his guitar and see him adjusting the volume of his amp.

Friday morning when I called, I was surprised to hear an unfamiliar voice on the line. I knew the whole rotation of nurses by now.

"I'm checking in on Roy Wilsing," I told the woman, assuming she was new.

She paused, and I presumed she was looking for his chart.

"There's no patient here by that name," she said.

My mouth dropped. *What?*

"I'm his daughter—Gina. I came there and saw him last week," I told her. "I've been calling every day for updates."

I heard a shuffling of papers.

"He passed away last night at eleven-fifteen," she said.

I was stunned.

It took a few seconds for me to respond. "Why didn't anyone call me?"

I imagined my dad lying in his hospital bed—knowing he was no longer there but not being able to process that he wasn't.

"It looks like two messages were left for your sister Tara," the woman said.

They should have called me, I wanted to say. *Why did they not call* me? I'd been waiting more than a week for that news, and I would have answered the phone. How sad that instead they'd had to leave a message—twice. As if no one cared he had died.

I thanked her for the update, hung up, and called Tara.

Why hadn't she called to tell me? Had she even heard her messages yet?

It turned out she had, just a short time before I'd called. She said she'd assumed the hospital had informed each of us. That made sense, but it didn't make me feel better. We hung up, and I called Clint to let him know our dad had passed. He said he'd tell Cliff.

I hung up and sat motionless at my kitchen table, the phone still in my hand. Even though I'd known it was coming, even though I'd called every day expecting him to be gone, it was still hard to believe he really was.

I missed him already. I missed the possibility of him ever again being in my life. Of him ever meeting my children. It may not have happened anyway, but now I knew for sure that it wouldn't.

I thought back to the seven of us standing around his bed at the hospital. I remembered some of the words the chaplain said and how we'd held hands. Despite my sadness, I was at peace with the decisions we'd made and relieved to know our dad was no longer suffering.

Later that day, the accident report was faxed to my home. It was all there in black and white—eleven pages of checklists and statements and diagrams.

A police officer had been a witness to the incident. At five o'clock that Tuesday evening, he'd been driving his patrol car north on Eighth Street, when to his left, he noticed our dad riding his bike on the sidewalk parallel to him. They were heading in the same direction, approaching the intersection of Eighth Street and Center Avenue. Up ahead to the officer's right, and also approaching the intersection, was a white Ford Taurus. It was heading west. It stopped at the stop sign. The officer stopped as well.

The driver of the Taurus was a fifty-five-year-old woman named Nancy. She'd left work early that day to get to the downtown post office before it closed. Her statement, in her handwriting, was included in the report.

I stopped and looked in all directions, she'd written, *and I noticed three ladies in the crosswalk. I waited for them to cross and again looked in all directions and did not see anyone else.*

The officer at the intersection verified that she'd made a complete stop. He then saw her drive through the intersection at a reasonable speed.

All of a sudden, Nancy had written, *I saw the bicycle and a man come onto my car and land on the hood and windshield.*

I gasped. Those words, written in her neat cursive letters, took me right to the scene. I knew those streets. I'd been at that intersection a hundred times. Peggy and I had taken the bus to and from that corner nearly every weekend when we were teenagers. It was in the middle of downtown, and on the corner was Security First National Bank, the tallest building in Sheboygan—the one my dad had said he'd hang his back brace on back in 1975. The Eighth Street Bridge was just a few blocks away, as was Grandma's house, right after you crossed over.

Temperatures were below freezing that Tuesday night. The report said my dad had been wearing a jacket but no gloves. *Why had he been out riding? Where had he been heading?*

He didn't stop at the curb, the officer reported. He just rode right into the street, outside of the crosswalk, and straight into the front left panel of Nancy's Taurus. He had no light on his bike, and the roads were wet from snow and ice, but the biggest factor contributing to the accident was my dad's blood alcohol level. A test run at the hospital an hour later would show he was heavily intoxicated.

A diagram included in the report showed an outline of his body in the middle of Center Avenue and his proximity to the car and his bicycle. Both the car and the bike were drawn twice—first using dashed lines, showing where they were at the time of impact, and then using solid lines, showing where the car had stopped and the bike had landed.

When I was done reading through the pages, I flipped back to Nancy's handwritten statement. From the answers she gave, I knew she lived in Sheboygan, she was married, and she lived three miles from where the accident had happened. My heart ached for her.

I assumed she felt guilty even though the accident hadn't been her fault. The report clearly stated it had been his. She couldn't have prevented it, but I was sure she felt she could've. Anyone would. She'd likely see flashes of him hitting her windshield her whole life long. She'd likely replay it in her mind a thousand times and wish she'd done something, *anything*, differently—stayed at work longer, taken a different route to the post office, seen him coming and slammed on her brakes before he'd crossed her path.

Living in Sheboygan, I imagined she'd seen the newspaper article, but I wondered if she knew that the man who'd run into her car had died. And wouldn't she want to know who he was? Wouldn't she want to know that his family was at peace? My guess was she would.

Her phone number was at the top of the page, and I knew I needed to dial it.

My heart pounded as I waited for her to answer. One ring, two rings, three . . . I hadn't planned what to say. I just felt there were things she needed to know.

"Hello?"

I hoped my words would make sense. "I'm Gina Wilsing," I said. "My father was the bicyclist who ran into your car."

She gasped.

I wanted to crawl through the line and hug her. I told her he'd passed away the night before.

"I'm so sorry," she said through tears.

I thanked her and went on to tell her about the life our dad had led—that he'd been homeless and an alcoholic and he hadn't had much of a relationship with any of his children. I told her that we went to Froedtert Hospital to be with him and that we'd taken him off life support. The accident, I said, brought us together for the first time ever. I told her we didn't blame her. We knew he was at fault.

"I'm so sorry this happened to you," I said. "I don't want you to feel bad."

She sighed. "You're taking this really well," she said.

"I just wanted you to know these things."

She thanked me profusely—for calling, for letting her know.

We'd talked for only a few minutes, but I felt worlds better when we hung up. I believe she did, too.

Five days later, on Christmas Eve, *The Sheboygan Press* published a second article about my dad's accident, headlined, "Bicyclist Dies of Injuries."

The first four paragraphs were about him, but the focus of the article was on the number of road fatalities that had occurred in Sheboygan County that year. My dad had been the eleventh traffic fatality in the county—the third within city limits.

Along with the statistics, safety measures were provided by the County Sheriff's Office and the Sheboygan Police Department. They reminded motorists to obey speed limits, wear seatbelts, and not drink and drive.

It would've been good if the report had also included

reminders of safety measures for bicyclists: obey city ordinances, wear a helmet, put a light on your bike, and again, don't drink and bike. I hoped the article would help people be more cautious. Maybe those tips would save a life. Maybe my dad's accident would serve as a warning to someone else.

The day after Christmas, Larry and I packed up the car and headed with the kids to our annual beach vacation in northwest Florida. We'd be gone for a week, leaving the Christmas tree up and the outdoor lights strung across the roof of the house. I wasn't thinking about my trip to Wisconsin or the papers I'd signed at the hospital or the call I'd made to the Sheboygan County Coroner's Office. Each hour I was at the coast with our family, thoughts of my dad drifted further away.

Our trip culminated with fireworks on New Year's Eve and football on New Year's Day. As Larry, the kids, and I made our two-hour trek back home the following day, I watched the scenery outside our car change from sand and sunshine to tall pines and then city streets. My thoughts moved from the fun we'd had with family to the beginning of our to-do list: ornaments off the tree, tree to the curb, groceries.

Larry turned onto our street and pulled into our driveway. My eyes went to the small, dark brown box sitting on our front porch. My to-do list fell away, and I pressed my hand to my heart.

"He's here." I looked at Larry.

He followed my eyes and slowed the car down to a stop. "Go ahead," he said, turning back to me.

I opened the door and stepped out, my body tingling down to my toes.

There he sat at my front door. How long had he been waiting for us to come home?

I paused for a moment and took in the size of the plastic

shipping container. It was no bigger than a shoebox, yet it held a whole life. My dad's life.

I sat down next to it, then heaved it up and cradled it like it was a stray cat—a fat, friendly, warm stray cat. I touched my fingers to his name and scoffed at an error someone had made on his birthdate. I read his date of death and wished once more that somehow I could've been there.

That January day, I thought our story had come to a close. I'd gone to Wisconsin, my dad had died, and his ashes had been sent to me. But as I sat in the stillness of the setting sun with him in my arms, an unsettling feeling came over me.

What do I do with him now?

I knew in my heart he should return to Wisconsin—to Sheboygan, our hometown—but I had no plans to go there any time soon. I knew I wanted to release his ashes with my siblings, but that wouldn't be possible for quite some time, given our distance and Cliff's remaining time in jail.

I looked down and smiled, realizing the temporary solution made me the happiest.

I'm going to keep you here with me for a while, I told my dad. I didn't know how long he would stay. I didn't have to figure it out right then. For now, it just felt right that he was with me.

I stood up and faced our front door.

Come on in, I said. *Make yourself at home.*

I walked through our house to the back room, the one I'd been working in when the call had come that Tuesday evening telling me my dad had been in an accident. I set his box on the closet floor, feeling thankful that I'd had the opportunity to be with him and my siblings at the hospital and feeling blessed to be the one who'd received his remains. I didn't know it would take me more than seven years to be ready to let him go.

CHAPTER 40

The Plans I Had

APRIL 2011

I kept my dad because keeping him made me feel close to him. It was as if he were with me—living my days with me, watching my children grow. I kept him because no part of me wanted to let him go after just getting him back.

I liked having custody over him and wasn't about to give up my rights.

Day after day, and then year after year, he sat in the same spot on my closet floor. To the left as I opened the doors, under three rows of shelving Larry had installed when we'd first moved in. Beneath boxes of holiday decorations, rolls of Christmas wrapping paper, and folders full of mementos from Ty's and Jillian's preschool and elementary-school years.

Though I went into the closet frequently, sometimes pausing, sometimes not, when the brown box caught my eye, its location never changed.

It remained unopened. Unmoved. Untouched.

During the several years before my dad's accident, when he hadn't reached out and I'd imagined someone calling to tell me he'd died, I'd thought I'd be okay with that news. I'd felt I'd done all I could and had made peace with our relationship. I'd thought I'd accepted his absence in my life and that his death wouldn't affect me.

Now that he was gone, I'd realized that wasn't true. His absence had made me love him even more and made me wish he and I had more time, even though I didn't know how anything would have been different if we had.

I didn't order a fancy urn or transfer his remains to a nicer container. He stayed in the original shipping box he'd arrived in. A nicer container wasn't necessary. I had no need to put him on display or even tell anyone he was there. His presence was all that mattered to me.

Besides, I knew I wouldn't keep him forever.

At times, I'd go into the closet and let my eyes linger on the box. I'd tell my dad the plans I had for him. Someday, when I felt ready, I knew just what I wanted to do.

I'll take you back to Sheboygan, I'd tell him. *I'll take you back to Cliff, Clint, and Tara.*

I hadn't been back to Wisconsin since the day I'd left Froedtert, and the four of us hadn't seen each other since the night we'd said goodbye in my hotel room. We'd kept in touch through letters and phone calls, but we had no plans to get together.

After our time at Froedtert, Cliff stayed in touch for the couple of years he was still in jail, but after his release, I hardly heard from him. He was living in Manitowoc, and I knew he'd lost the rights to his children, but on the rare occasions we spoke, he didn't share much about his life. I hoped he'd find his footing, and it saddened me that he seemed so lost. Clint told me he'd tried to help, but eventually, he'd had to leave Cliff to his own devices.

Soon after our reunion at the hospital, Clint started taking classes at the local college in Manitowoc and earned his A.A.

degree. He began working in home renovation, and he and his girlfriend, Lindsey, had a baby girl. He'd found ways to move forward, and he'd started a family of his own. I was happy for him.

He and Tara had gotten together a few times over the years. She was still living in Sheboygan with her mom and stepdad and was working as an in-home caregiver for the elderly. She'd always enjoyed helping people, and I was thrilled she'd found a profession she loved.

Someday, I'd tell our dad, *someday, we'll all be together again.*

I pictured Cliff, Clint, Tara, and myself standing on the Sheboygan pier on the shore of Lake Michigan. It was my hope that we'd open the box and release our dad's ashes together. I imagined him flying into the wind and riding the waves from the big lake into the Sheboygan River. He'd head toward the Eighth Street Bridge—of course he would—and I just knew that a tall boat would come along at the same moment he was passing under. The drawbridge would open as the boat glided through, and up on Eighth Street, the bells would clang, and the red lights would flash—welcoming our dad back home.

Someday.

Most times when I thought about that day, I assumed it would be far in the future, when my kids were older, and Larry and I could easily afford the trip. Scattering my dad's ashes anywhere other than our hometown wouldn't feel right. It had to be there, and I had to be with my siblings.

I could wait. My heart was in no hurry.

Then one day, in the spring of 2011, an invitation popped up on my Facebook feed.

Join the Class of 1986 for our twenty-fifth reunion!

I froze at the sight of it. It was planned for that August, just four months away. Ty, Jillian, and I all had the summer off. They were finishing the fifth and third grades, respectively, and

I was a teacher at their school. We had the time to go. Larry and I were doing fine financially. We had the money to make it possible.

I hadn't been back to Sheboygan in fifteen years, not since my ten-year reunion, and the idea of going was exciting. I'd get to see Peggy and lots of old friends. I'd get to visit my brothers and sister, see my aunts Eunice and Dorothy.

But if I went home, if I went back, how could I not bring my dad's remains? How could I go home and not bring *him* home, too? I set my phone down on the kitchen table and went to our back office. I opened the closet doors and stood staring at the box on the floor.

Was it time? Was the universe calling my bluff, or had I really just been waiting for the right moment? There was nothing holding me back except my need to keep things exactly as they were.

I sat down next to the box and rested my hand on the mailing labels. I reread his birthdate, the date I'd corrected when I'd first received the box, and I ran my finger along his name. *Roy Earl Wilsing.*

A feverish heat flushed through me. My chest felt tight.

Could I let him go? Did I have to?

I closed the bifold doors, bit my lip, and rested my head against the panel in front of me.

His remains were all I had of him.

He'd had no possessions. No home to go through or sell. No clothing to keep or donate. No keepsakes. I didn't even know what had happened to his family photo album. And I'd given away every gift he'd ever given me except for my silver charm bracelet. I had pictures of him and the letters he'd written to me, but I had nothing that had belonged to him. How could I let go of his ashes when they were the only part of him I'd been able to keep?

There was a reason I hadn't opened that box. A reason why

I hadn't moved it or touched it. I'd wanted everything to stay just the way it was. I'd wanted my dad to stay just the way he'd come to me. If I did nothing with his ashes, if everything remained intact, then maybe my heart would too. If I kept the box here with me, I'd never really have to say goodbye to my dad. He'd always be with me. And I needed him to stay.

I went back to the kitchen and called Peggy. She was going to the reunion, she said, and of course she wanted me to come. I called a few old friends and asked if they'd be in town. They would be, and they were excited I was thinking about making the trip. I called Cliff, Clint, and Tara. Cliff said he'd be around. Clint was excited I'd get to meet his girlfriend and their daughter, Layla. I talked with Larry and mentioned maybe doing a road trip. Maybe taking Ty and Jillian. They'd never been to my hometown and had never met Cliff, Clint, or Tara. Tara said she'd get the weekend off, and she'd babysit while Larry and I went to my reunion.

The planets were aligning, and it seemed the universe was asking me to be strong.

I went to the closet, opened its doors, and sat again on the floor facing the box that had appeared on my front porch between Christmas 2003 and New Year's Day 2004.

It wasn't lost on me that the seven years I'd kept my dad in my closet was equal to the length of time he and I had gone without speaking before his death. Maybe I'd needed every minute of those seven years to feel like I'd regained the time we'd been apart. Maybe it was no coincidence that my invitation to come home had arrived at this time.

CHAPTER 41

The Rock

AUGUST 2011

On the first Friday in August, one day before my twenty-fifth high-school reunion, Larry, the kids, my dad, and I arrived in Sheboygan. I looked forward to reuniting with my friends and family and was excited about sharing my hometown with Ty and Jillian. I was also ready to see Cliff, Clint, and Tara and feeling good about releasing our dad's ashes.

We would do that on Sunday, we'd decided, in Manitowoc. Cliff had to work, so it was best to do it there. That would give us more time together. My vision of our dad floating under the Eighth Street Bridge in Sheboygan became a little cloudy, but I held out hope that somehow I could make both things happen.

The most important thing, of course, was for me and my siblings to reunite and for the four of us to scatter the ashes together.

Manitowoc was, in its own way, another special place in our dad's life. He'd lived there in his twenties with my mom and me shortly after I was born. He'd started his own business there, and he'd owned his own home. And maybe Manitowoc was best for Cliff and Clint. They'd lived there most of their lives and still did. Our dad would now be close to them.

Saturday, the day of the reunion, Tara, Clint, and his daughter, Layla, met up with us at the hotel where we were staying with Peggy. We spent the afternoon together at the Bratwurst Day festival, an annual hometown event I'd enjoyed going to many times as a child and teen. Ty, Jillian, and four-year-old Layla quickly connected, running around in the sunshine and giggling over which carnival rides to go on. The rest of us enjoyed the bratwurst and beer and each other's company. It was as if no time had gone by. Cliff hadn't been able to make it. He was working, he said, but he'd see us Sunday for sure.

Saturday night, Tara stayed with the kids while Peggy, Larry, and I enjoyed the reunion.

Sunday morning, Peggy headed home. She had a prior engagement and couldn't spend the day with us. We picked up Tara and made two stops on our way to Manitowoc—one to take pictures of Ty and Jillian in front of my childhood home and the other to visit my Aunt Eunice.

That weekend, Eunice happened to be staying at her family's lake house, where I'd spent many summer days as a child. It was one of my favorite places. I was excited that Larry, Ty, and Jillian would get to enjoy it, and so happy that Tara was with us. Eunice hadn't seen her since she was a baby.

While Ty and Jillian splashed around in the lake and tried out the kayaks, Eunice showed Tara and me pictures from summers past, when everyone in the family would get together at the lake house on the weekends. There was a picture of our dad playing guitar right where we were sitting and another picture of me with my many cousins. I could've stayed all day, and Ty and Jillian would've loved that, but we had lunch to get to and ashes to scatter.

"Your dad was a good guy," Eunice said as she hugged me goodbye.

I looked into her eyes and knew she meant it.

"It was the alcohol that changed him," she said softly. "It's too bad what happened."

We'd never spoken about it before, and I appreciated her sentiment.

"Thank you for being there for him," I said and kissed her on the cheek.

We got back on the road, and I picked up the phone to call Clint. We hadn't yet decided where to meet for lunch. I'd just told him that Larry and I wanted to take the kids somewhere local. I was about to punch in his number when the phone rang in my hand. It was my mom calling to check in on us. She was a local, too, so I asked her.

"Oh, you should go to Late's!" she said without hesitation.

"Is that the name of a restaurant?"

She laughed and told me it had been around since she was in high school. "They have the best pizzaburgers and malts, and the kids would *love* their fried cheese curds!"

I thanked her, hung up, and called Clint.

"Are you almost here?" He sounded excited and told me Lindsey and Layla would be coming to lunch with us.

"Yes, and—" I was going to share my mom's restaurant suggestion.

"I know where we should go," he said before I could. "Late's! It's been around forever, and they have the best fried cheese curds."

I couldn't help but smile. "We'll see you there!" I said.

Thirty minutes later, we pulled up to what looked like a malt shop from the 1950s, and the moment I opened the van door, I knew why this was the restaurant that we'd had to come to. I immediately recognized the famous voice singing, "The Wonder of You." It blared from the outdoor speakers mounted on the roof.

Tara's eyes lit up as she hopped out of the van. "That's my favorite Elvis song!" she squealed. She took off toward the restaurant with Ty and Jillian each holding one of her hands.

Of course it is, I thought.

Our dad's proper sendoff had begun.

Clint, Lindsey, and Layla arrived, and our group filled all the bar stools around the diner's horseshoe-shaped counter. Jillian and Layla flanked Tara like little chicks nestling near a mother hen, and Ty sat on Layla's other side. We saved a stool for Cliff, but he called shortly after we ordered to say he'd meet up with us after lunch. I was disappointed but not surprised. Clint told him we'd call when we knew where we were headed next.

We didn't go far. Lake Michigan was just a short walk away, past a children's playground across the street from the restaurant. We could see the white tips of the waves just beyond the merry-go-round.

"Wanna walk over there?" Clint asked.

I did. And I wanted to make sure Cliff would find us.

Clint said he'd call him.

I went to the van to retrieve our dad's remains. The heat from the summer sun had warmed the plastic box, and I was reminded of how it had felt to cradle it in my arms when I'd first received it. Holding it carefully, I walked across the street to Red Arrow Park, a name I recognized from my childhood photo album.

"I have pictures of myself playing here when I was little," I told Larry. I'd been about three years old.

Clint hung up his phone and nodded at the box in my arms. It was the first time he'd seen it. He reached for it, and I gave it to him to carry. He stood still and held it for a moment before moving toward the water.

I looked through the trees toward the lake. It was a perfect day. The sky was clear and the temperature was in the low seventies.

"Hey," Clint turned back to look at me. "Do you think I could have some of this?"

Some of our dad? "Sure, of course."

"Okay, thanks." He turned back around and continued walking, and I realized he'd taken a Styrofoam cup and plastic spoon from Late's in the hopes that I'd say yes.

I was happy he'd asked. He wanted to keep our dad for a while, too. Maybe forever. I got that.

Our group reached the shore. Layla stood between her mother and Tara and took each of their hands. Ty and Jillian followed behind them. Larry took pictures of us every step of the way. I was used to him documenting our lives, and I was grateful we'd have pictures of this momentous day.

I turned back toward the park, hoping I'd see Cliff.

I didn't.

Is he on his way? Will he be able to find us? Will he come at all?

My next steps would take the park out of my sightline. I moved forward and caught up with the others, hoping Cliff would be there soon.

It wasn't long before Tara and the kids kicked off their flip flops. They squished wet sand through their toes in the ankle-deep pools of water near the shoreline. Clint, Lindsey, and Layla followed along as our group moved south toward a more secluded area. I fell in behind them, continuing to look over my shoulder for Cliff.

Tara and the kids dipped their feet into the lake water. The surprised look on Jillian's face told me it wasn't the temperature of the tropical water she was used to. Ty went in knee-deep, pulling his shorts up high on his thighs, as if they wouldn't be soaked by the end of the afternoon. I laughed, readjusted the clip in my hair to keep wisps from flying in my face, and glanced back toward the park.

Cliff was walking down the shore in our direction.

I waved my arm, overcome with relief, and ran to meet him halfway. We embraced, neither of us saying a word. His eyes told me he was strung out. I didn't know on what. But he was here, and I was so glad he'd come.

We joined the rest of the group, and Clint handed Cliff the box. He stood staring at it for a long while and hung on to it as we walked down the beach together.

In front of us, Ty stopped and pointed to a pair of boulders sticking out of the water several yards ahead.

"Can I swim out to those?" Ty asked.

"Sure!" Larry chimed in from behind his camera lens. "Go climb on top of one—that'll make a great picture."

Ty shot out into the lake with Tara right behind him. Jillian, dressed in pink shorts and a t-shirt, with a baseball cap on backwards, followed suit.

"That looks like fun!" Clint kicked off his flip flops and headed in.

"Hey," I yelled out at them. "What if . . . What if the four of us go out there? What if we—"

Tara and Clint, halfway there already, turned back to look at me.

"Yeah!" Clint said. He turned and headed to the largest of the two boulders.

Cliff handed me our dad's box. He pulled off his tennis shoes and threw them on the sand.

"Okay!" I kicked off my sandals. "Let's do this!"

Ty and Jillian made their way back to shore as Cliff and I walked hand-in-hand past them toward the rock. I held our dad's box close to my chest until I was waist deep, then held it up for Clint to take. He was almost to the top of the rock. He set the box in a secure spot, then turned to help the three of us climb up. There was just enough room on the boulder for the four of us.

"Let's get a picture!" Larry yelled from the shore, and we turned to face him, posing in our sopping wet clothes—serendipitously in birth order. I smiled for the camera, feeling joyful that we were together and ready to move forward in saying goodbye to our dad.

No one had questioned why it had taken me so long to return to Wisconsin with him. No one judged me for keeping him to myself. We had each needed time to process what had happened in our personal relationships with our dad and during our time at Froedtert.

The four of us sat down on the boulder and looked at each other, unsure of how to begin.

Clint lifted the box, and I handed him a small, serrated knife I'd brought from home just for this purpose. I watched as he carefully sawed into the white duct tape at the edge. He stopped short of lifting the lid and looked my way. Cliff and Tara turned to me as well. They were waiting for me to begin.

My favorite memories, the ones I'd told my dad that day at Froedtert, came to mind. So instead of starting with a prayer or saying something profound, I shared those. It felt good to share the dad I knew. It made me happy when they laughed at the jokes I remembered him telling. They'd missed out on knowing that side of him.

Cliff talked about how it had felt to reunite with our dad when he'd turned eighteen. He'd hoped for more of a relationship but was glad that at least they'd met and hung out a few times. Tara said she was so grateful we'd all gone to Froedtert. She wouldn't have gone alone, she said, and she would've regretted that.

Clint offered to say a prayer. He set the box between himself and Cliff, and the four of us held hands as Clint spoke.

When he finished, we sat still for a moment. Then Clint picked up the box and opened the lid.

I watched as he lifted out a clear plastic bag. During all the years I'd had my dad's box in my closet, I hadn't thought about what his remains would look like. Though the box had been heavier than I'd expected it to be when I'd seen the size of it, I still thought of his remains as just ashes. Ashes to ashes and dust to dust. What I saw now in the plastic bag looked more like small bits of gravel. Small bits of bone. I knew what it really was—pieces of our dad. All that was left.

My fingertips went to my lips, and I blinked back tears. It was time to let him go.

Clint set the box on the rock near his feet, steadied the bag in his hands, and held it in my direction.

He expects me to go first.

I had thought I'd be ready.

But I wasn't.

I looked down the line at the four of us standing barefoot on the rock.

Four of us.

"I want to go last," I said. I looked at Tara who was standing next to Clint. "Would you go first?"

She nodded and took the bag in her hands. In the order we were standing, we'd release our dad's remains from youngest to oldest.

Cliff slipped his arm around my waist as Clint untwisted the plastic at the top of the bag and opened it. I put my arm around Cliff's shoulder, and the three of us watched as Tara tipped the open end toward the waves below.

As the first pieces fell, an enormous flock of seagulls took flight above us, their white wings in stark contrast to the bright blue sky. I watched them fly away and felt a tremendous sense of relief building within me. The world was shifting as our dad was returning to it, and I knew that everything was going to be okay. It was as it should be. I had nothing to be afraid of.

His remains floated away in the wind and fell into the water. He rode with the waves. He was now, and forever would be, part of something larger than himself. And at the same time, he was free.

Tara handed the bag to Clint and wiped her eyes. Clint took his turn and handed the bag to Cliff who did the same.

I reached out to take it, noticing it was still half full. I'd release most of his ashes here, but I remembered Clint wanted some, and I still wanted to take my dad to Sheboygan. It was important that part of him remained there—important to me, and I knew that if he'd had a say, it would've been important to him.

I bit the inside of my lip, tilted the bag, and stared at the gravelly mix of bone and powder as it fell into the lake. When there were about two cups left, I stopped pouring. I twisted the plastic bag shut, and Cliff opened the box for me to set it back inside. Then the four of us joined in a family hug on the middle of the rock. I couldn't have imagined anything better.

I thought about how we'd come to this moment. How our dad's accident had brought the four of us together. A day earlier, when Larry and I had been in Sheboygan, I'd stood at the intersection of Eighth Street and Center Avenue, in the exact spot where our dad had landed after hitting the car. I'd needed to go there, to Point A, the beginning of the end. I'd needed to see it for myself after picturing it in my mind a hundred times. I thought of the phone call I'd received that December night, how shocking it had been to learn I was expected at the hospital. I realized my time in counseling had helped me not only come to terms with my past, but it had prepared me for a future I'd never dreamed of.

During my teenage years, I'd built a wall to protect myself. I'd had every right to. But the counseling and the retreats I'd attended in my twenties had helped me let go of the defenses that were no longer serving me. They helped me create an opening through which I could see things more clearly. Through which I could reach out.

That had helped me find the strength to build a bridge, but when my dad didn't cross it—didn't take the opportunity to stay connected—I didn't understand.

It turned out I'd be the one needing to cross it. In order to be next of kin, I'd had to walk across that bridge I'd built. Test its stability. Trust it would hold.

Had I not created the opening in the first place, had I not realized my own strength, I would not have gone to Froedtert.

But I had, and I did.

I went to take care of him, but by going, I also took care of myself. I went because I was needed, but it was also where I needed to be.

I looked at my siblings standing with me on the rock and thought of how we'd all benefitted because I'd decided to go, and just as quickly, I realized that wasn't true. I hadn't been the only one who'd made this happen. It had taken each of us being willing, being open, being strong. We'd each had our own bridge to cross. And each of us had.

Cliff walked to the edge and looked out into the vast blue sky. Clint took the box, and he and Tara slid back into the water and waded toward Lindsey and Layla on the shore. Larry waved to me, camera in hand, and I smiled for a picture.

"Hey, Mom!" Ty yelled over the waves as he and Jillian ran back into the water. They were heading in my direction.

I glanced at Cliff who seemed lost in thought. I prayed he'd be okay.

"Let's go to the other rock," I yelled to Ty. I slid down and swam toward it, reaching it before he and Jillian did. I climbed to the top and found my balance on the wet boulder.

Alone for a moment, I tilted back my head and closed my

eyes. The sun kissed my face and a light breeze blew through my hair. I thought of Elvis' voice and the stories I'd told and the prayer Clint had shared. We'd gathered. We'd celebrated our dad's life, and together, we'd set him free.

I'd set myself free, too. I'd kept my dad for so long because I didn't want to be without him. Now I understood I never would be. I didn't need the box. I didn't need his remains. He would live on in me—and Cliff and Clint and Tara—and we all had each other. Our dad's ashes weren't all that remained of him.

I opened my eyes and watched the sunlight dance on the water. I followed the waves and thought of how he rode them. I felt the wind and imagined all the places our dad would now go.

Far from losing him, we'd simply released him back to the universe where now he'd be with us every step of the way.

I took a breath. Was I breathing him in? I turned my face back to the sun and raised my hands to the sky, palms up.

I could feel my dad's presence, and it felt like love.

CHAPTER 42
Going Back Home

AUGUST 2011

Just a few short hours after my siblings and I released most of our dad's ashes in Manitowoc, I took the remaining two cups to Sheboygan where I sent half of them floating down Lake Michigan toward the Eighth Street Bridge, just like I'd wanted to. The other half I took to a place my dad had never been to but surely would've wanted to go.

On our way home from Wisconsin, Larry and I planned to spend a night in Memphis, and I decided I couldn't be that close to Graceland without taking my dad there, too.

We didn't have time to take a tour, but as luck—or fate—would have it, the morning we pulled up to the entrance of Elvis's mansion, just to see what might be possible, the wrought-iron gates opened for a tour bus, and I was able to sneak onto the property. I slipped behind an old oak tree, plastic bag in hand, and began to discreetly sprinkle my dad's remains.

He sold three hundred and twelve million albums! I could hear my dad's voice my head. I could see his face and picture him handing me the Elvis mirror he'd just won. *He was the greatest. He was the King!*

I would've left the rest of my dad's remains right there had I not been run off by a wild-eyed security guard shouting that I needed permission to scatter ashes on the grounds. I shot out of the gate as she headed to call for reinforcements. I'd managed to sprinkle some and was thrilled that part of my dad would always be there, legally or not.

Having half a cup left, part of him would be going back home with me, too. After everything we'd been through, that seemed exactly as it should be.

The sun was just setting as we arrived home that evening. Large swaths of orange and pink clouds were spread across the sky. As we pulled into the driveway, my eyes went to our front porch, to the place I'd first seen my dad's brown box, and then down to where it now rested at my feet, holding the plastic bag with the last of his remains.

Larry pulled into the garage, the kids unbuckled, and I picked up the container from the floor. I wasn't about to put him back in my closet. I was moving nowhere but forward.

I walked to the flower garden on the side of our house, opened the box, and took out the bag. The tri-colored blossoms of our lantana bushes were in full bloom, and the tiny clusters of bright yellow, orange, and red petals made me smile.

There had been no service for our dad until Cliff, Clint, Tara, and I met on the rock.

There'd been no music but then we heard Elvis sing at Late's.

There'd been no flowers, but now there were these.

And he was with me. He would always be with me.

Epilogue

MAY 2023

When I wrote the first lines of this book, my dad was still in my closet. I'd just received the invitation to go home for my reunion. I didn't know I'd gather at the rock with my siblings. I didn't know it would be the beginning of a deeper connection for all of us.

While our dad's death had brought the four of us together for the first time, it was our meeting at the rock—our second time together after seven years of letters and phone calls—that solidified our relationships with each other. Since that day, Larry, Ty, Jillian, and I have made numerous trips back to Sheboygan and Manitowoc, and each of my siblings has stayed with us at our home in Tallahassee. Beyond simply seeing each other more often, every gathering has brought us all closer. We're now growing up together—as adults. Our significant others know each other, as do our children. We are family. And that is one of the greatest blessings of my life.

Cliff's recovery has been a blessing as well. A year after the four of us released our dad's ashes, Cliff was encouraged by family to seek help for his addictions. He reconnected with a childhood sweetheart, Christma, who was in recovery and working in juvenile justice. With Christma's help, Cliff took his first steps toward sobriety, and as of this writing, he's been clean for eleven years.

A year into his recovery, he reunited with his children, Dontae and Jade. They're now in their mid-twenties. Jade recently moved back to Wisconsin and lives with Erin. Dontae works for Cliff, doing home construction for a company Cliff started several years ago.

In 2007, he and Christma married. Together, they are raising her daughter Aria, who just turned thirteen, and they've fostered children through the years.

Along with Christma, Cliff helped found Lighthouse Recovery Community Center, a non-profit recovery center in Manitowoc. He serves in the role of recovery support specialist, helping others on their recovery journey. Today, Christma is the director of the center, and Cliff continues to support the efforts of their mission.

In the near future, Cliff and Christma plan to build a home on property they own just north of Manitowoc. They will be just a few short miles from where Clint and Lindsey bought their first home a year ago.

Clint and I talk a couple of times a month, mostly about parenthood. His daughter, Layla, is now sixteen, and Ty and Jillian are in their early twenties, so there's always a lot to share. His knowledge of my relationship with our dad has made him especially sensitive to how precious his relationship with Layla is. He's always been a good father, coaching her in softball from a young age and being present for important moments in her life. Most importantly, he listens to her. He's one of the best dads I know.

And then there's Tara. In the aftermath of seeing our dad at Froedtert and releasing his ashes with us, she struggled to work through her feelings about the father who'd abandoned her. For the past four years, she has witnessed her partner Dale's dedication to his three children and has further questioned how her own father could have given her up. Tara has always been one to help others, especially the elderly and the young, and in April of 2023 she was blessed with a child of her own. I'll get to meet little Ava this fall when I travel back to my hometown. After years of wanting a child, I know Tara will be a loving mother, and I couldn't be happier for her.

As for me, the last twelve years have been filled with pursuing my greatest passions—enjoying life with Larry (we recently celebrated our twenty-sixth anniversary); raising our children, who are now in college; teaching fourth grade, until I switched careers during the pandemic; and writing this book.

In my research for the book, I learned things I never would've known otherwise.

From the hospital report I ordered eight years after our dad's death, I learned he'd had his wallet on him at the time of his accident. The contents of which included his Wisconsin ID card, a Target card, an MCI calling card, and twenty-five dollars and seventy-three cents. I called to ask if they still had it. They didn't, but they let me know that any gift cards or money left behind went to a charity to buy Christmas gifts for children in the hospital.

From the organ donation records, I learned our dad had alcohol-induced dementia. He'd had it for years. That explained a lot.

From the police records I reread, I realized there were photos taken the night of the accident. I visited the police station on one of my trips to Sheboygan and standing at the entrance was an officer whose name I recognized. It was on his badge, and it had been on the police report.

"You probably don't remember this," I said as I introduced

myself, "but you were at the scene of an accident that involved my dad."

Not only did he remember, but he told me he uses my dad's story as a cautionary tale for bicyclists. I hope that saves at least one life.

As I write this closing, I'm looking forward to truly letting go. This has been a long journey, but one I will be forever grateful I took. I get that, ironically, this book will replace my dad's brown box, but I'm okay with that. And I won't keep it in my closet.

I long ago accepted the pieces of our relationship that I know I could not have changed. I found the courage to do the things I needed to do at the end of his life. And I gained the wisdom that you can get only when you choose to forgive.

Rest in peace, Dad. Rest in peace.

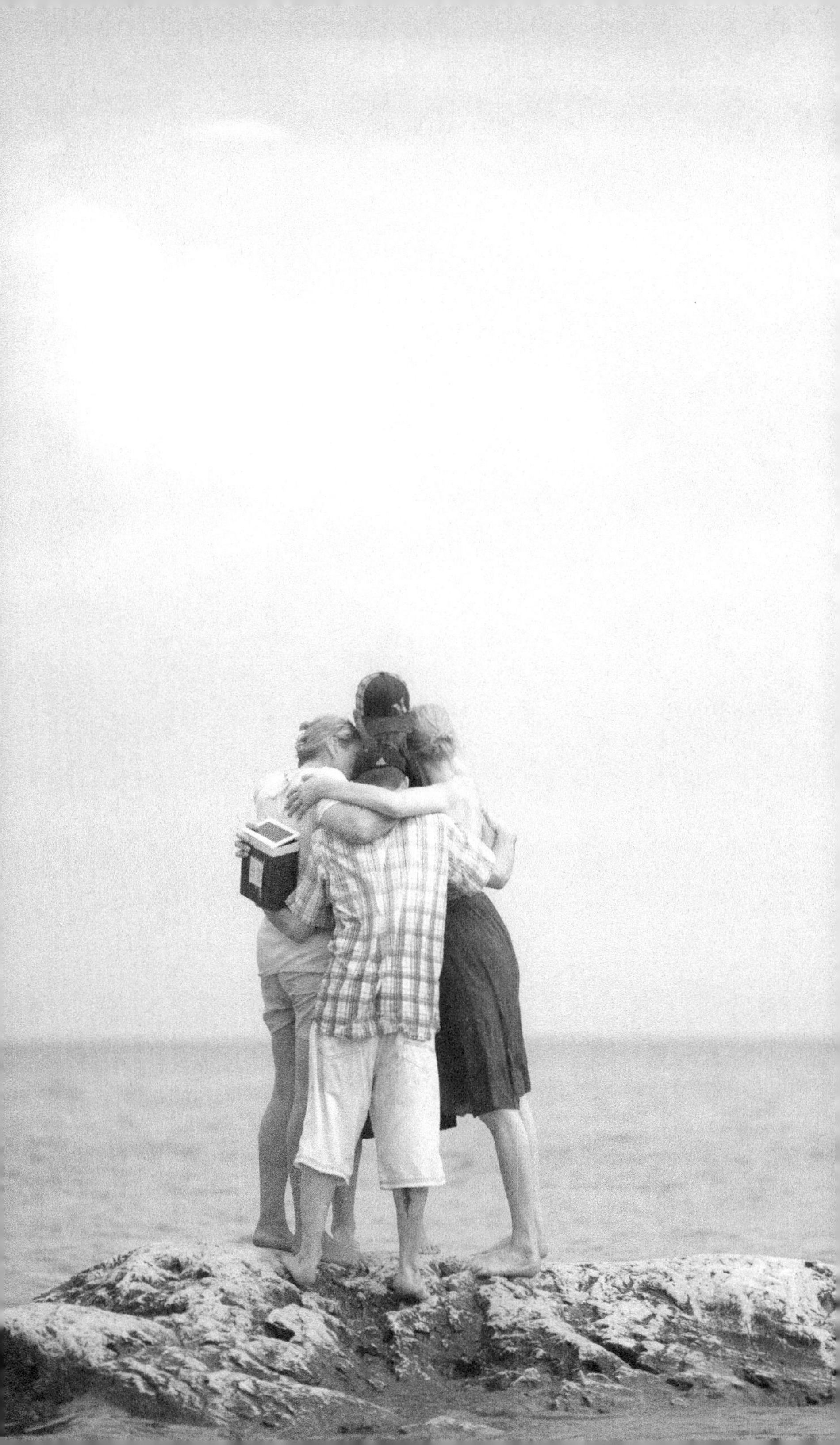

In Memoriam
Twenty years later

Roy Earl Wilsing, 59, a longtime resident of Sheboygan, Wisconsin, passed away December 18, 2003, at Froedtert Hospital in Milwaukee. Roy was born July 19, 1944, to the late William Wilsing, Jr., and Florence Chapaton Wilsing.

He graduated from Sheboygan South High School in 1963 and worked as a carpet installer for thirty-three years. Roy came from a musical family and from a young age enjoyed playing guitar and singing. He was a people person who always had a smile on his face and a joke to tell. He loved playing baseball, shooting pool, and bowling.

Roy at the age of twenty-four

Survivors include two daughters, Gina and Tara; two sons, Cliff and Clint; four grandchildren, Dontae, Jade, Ty, and Jillian; two sisters-in-law, Eunice and Dorothy; and several nieces and nephews.

He was preceded in death by his parents and three brothers, Earl, Roger "Buddy," and Terry.

Roy's remains were scattered by his daughters and sons in August 2011 in a private ceremony on the shore of Lake Michigan in Manitowoc. A family gathering is being planned for Fall 2023 to celebrate his life and recognize the twentieth anniversary of his death.

Resources

Lighthouse Recovery Community Center
If you or someone you know is struggling with substance-use disorder, help is available. In the United States, call or text (920) 374-3989 for free, 24/7, confidential support. https://lighthouserecoverycommunitycenter.org/

Substance Abuse and Mental Health Services
The national helpline for the Substance Abuse and Mental Health Services Administration, 1-800-662-HELP (4357), is free, confidential, and available 24/7, 365 days a year. They provide information for individuals and family members facing mental and/or substance-use disorders. This service also provides referrals to local treatment facilities, support groups, and community-based organizations.
https://www.samhsa.gov/find-help/national-helpline

The Salvation Army
An international organization dedicated to helping people in need—from homeless shelters to rehabilitation to job training and more. https://www.salvationarmyusa.org/usn/

Alcoholics Anonymous

A recovery program based on one alcoholic helping another. https://www.aa.org/

Al-Anon/Alateen

For those who are worried about someone with a drinking problem. https://al-anon.org/

Narcotics Anonymous

For those who have found that drugs have become a major problem. A recovery program in which addicts help each other stay clean. https://na.org/

Organ Donation

Learn about the process of organ donation and how to become a donor. https://www.organdonor.gov/

***Life 101: Everything We Wish We Had Learned About Life in School—But Didn't*,** by Peter McWilliams

***Homecoming: Reclaiming and Championing Your Inner Child*,** by John Bradshaw

Global Relationship Centers

This was the name of the organization through which I took the course, *Understanding Yourself and Others*. Versions of this course are now taught under different organizational names throughout the United States. If you search for Global Relationship Centers, you may find one near you. I encourage you to go. It is one of the best things I ever did for myself.

Acknowledgments

A book is not the work of any one person. I am forever indebted to all those who helped make this one possible.

To Beth McGrotha—your interest in my story made me believe it was worth telling, and your abundant enthusiasm inspired me to sit down and write the very first lines.

To Heather Whitaker, my brilliant writing coach, content editor, and the founder of Red Pen Writers—without your guidance and encouragement, I surely would have crawled into a hole before getting to end of my final manuscript. Thank you for your dedication, time, and energy (and thank you to Geoff for sharing you).

To all my Red Pen peeps—your love and support means the world to me. Thank you for propelling me forward, calming my fears, and giving me a safe space in which to be myself. To my writing partner Mary Bowers, our weekly meetings were invaluable, and your insights helped make every chapter better. To Lipika Frith, thank you for your gentle perspective on life and your tiny but mighty line edits. To Aide Whitaker and Jessica Thompson, thank you for being early readers in the beginning and proofreaders at the end. To my copy editor Liz Jameson, how lucky I am to have met you when I was just starting out. Thank you for sharing your knowledge, your books, and your home with all of us.

To Angel Kalafatis, Brandon Waller, Christma Rusch, Justin White, and Peggy Kisiolek—thank you for your delight in proofing this prior to publication and for your valuable feedback.

To Larry—most importantly, thank you for loving me through everything. *I think I got the best one!* Thank you for listening to my ideas and for letting me talk things out. Thank you for reading and editing the manuscripts, and for documenting our lives in pictures, which helped so much in remembering every detail of our day on the rock. And thank you for the many groceries you shopped for and the many dinners you made, allowing me more time to work on this project of my heart.

To Ty and Julia—your encouragement every step of the way has been a blessing. What an amazing experience to have you read and edit all the versions over all these years. Thank you for sharing this experience with me. Ty, I wish you joy as you journey further into the world of words, and Julia, in addition to your valuable insights, I thank you for your beautiful book design. I feel like my story is wrapped in love.

To Jillian—thank you for your support. I'm excited that you can finally hold this book in your hands and read it. You can analyze me after you get your Psych degree. I love you, and I'm so happy you have such a wonderful dad.

To my mother, Sharon—thank you for always being there for me and for continually reminding me how much I am loved. I didn't anticipate us working on this book together, but now I can't imagine it having happened any other way. I know your heart is in every chapter, and I know you loved him too.

To Cliff, Clint, and Tara—you are in my heart, always. Thank you for giving me the freedom to write this book and for your support along the way. Thank you for loving me and thank you for letting me love you.

About the Author

Gina Beth (Wilsing) Davidson was born in Sheboygan, Wisconsin. She received her bachelor's degree in secondary English education from Florida State University and has been a freelance writer for more than thirty years. In addition to co-authoring a book and writing for publication, she taught language arts at the high-school and elementary-school levels for eleven years.

Her work has appeared in several newspapers, including the *Charlotte Sun*, *Tallahassee Democrat*, and *Charlotte Observer*, as well as magazines, including *Tallahassee, Unconquered,* and *Sandestin*. Gina lives in Tallahassee, Florida, with her husband, Larry, and their thirteen-year-old golden retriever, Clark. She can be reached at ginabdavidson@gmail.com.

Made in United States
Orlando, FL
13 November 2023